The Relate Guide to Sex and Intimacy

CATE CAMPBELL

MA, PGDip PST, MCOSRT (Accred), MBACP (Accred)

relate
the relationship people

Vermilion
LONDON

1 3 5 7 9 10 8 6 4 2

Vermilion, an imprint of Ebury Publishing,
20 Vauxhall Bridge Road,
London SW1V 2SA

Vermilion is part of the Penguin Random House group of companies whose
addresses can be found at global.penguinrandomhouse.com

Penguin
Random House
UK

First published by Vermilion in 2015

www.eburypublishing.co.uk

A CIP catalogue record for this book is available from the British Library

ISBN 9781785040078

Printed and bound in Great Britain by Clays Ltd, St Ives PLC

Penguin Random House is committed to a sustainable future
for our business, our readers and our planet. This book is made
from Forest Stewardship Council® certified paper.

Contents

PART FOUR:
MAINTAINING AND IMPROVING YOUR SEX LIFE

Introduction

We all have times in our lives when sex and intimacy are great and other times when either we aren't interested or sex isn't so interesting. This isn't something most of us talk about. When we do, we start to measure our sex lives against other people's and then either can't understand why our partner is so dissatisfied or feel there is something wrong with us.

This book will address what might be considered sexual problems and why they happen; it will also help you to celebrate your sexuality, discover or enhance your sexual self and maintain a comfortable level of intimacy within your relationship. It will equip you to manage sexual and intimacy matters not just now but in the future, anticipating circumstances and relationship issues that you may encounter as your life together evolves so you will never be unprepared.

Though fictitious, the case examples included are typical of Relate's real clients. Exercises, quizzes and talking points feature throughout to help you make the most of the information. Though the chapters build on each other as the book progresses, you can easily dip in and out to find the information you need.

The first part of the book, **Understanding Sex and Desire**, opens by explaining why we need intimacy in our lives and what that actually means. Taking a contemporary look at hopes and expectations for our relationships, it considers what helps and hinders our sense of intimacy, expression of our sexuality and our comfort with this. Acknowledging that there are more pressures than ever on couple relationships, it considers how we negotiate our way through modern stresses and misunderstandings to get what we want and need from our sex lives. Chapter One, *Why Intimacy is Important*, looks at the benefits of sex and intimacy for our health and overall wellbeing. This chapter also begins to explore how desire can sometimes become a barrier to intimacy rather than a route to pleasure; if you feel your partner wants more or less sex than you do, you may worry that you will never find a comfortable sexual fit which satisfies you both. This theme is picked up in the following chapter on *Gender Differences*, which explains why you may perceive your sexual appetite differently from your partner, not only in straight relationships but when you are a same-sex couple, answering some of the questions about why your partner may sometimes be such a mystery. Part One concludes by considering how all this affects *Your Sexual Image* and how you express your sexuality. Whether you have ever wished you felt sexier or are already entirely comfortable with your sexual expression, this will help you to enjoy, enhance and maintain the expression of your sexual self.

Sexual Coupledom is the subject of Part Two, investigating how the early days of our relationships influence their future and how we can develop intimacy behaviours and habits that we may relish or regret. Though we may be nostalgic about this time, wondering why it couldn't last, the opening chapter on *Keeping Your Relationship Alive* explains why those early days can't be recaptured. The challenges involved in developing a more settled, deeper and lasting bond are examined, along with how we develop as individuals without relying too much on the affirmation of our partner.

Lasting solutions may need a bit of work, however, as the longer we know each other the more powerfully our sexual scripts can kick in, as the next chapter, *The Sexual Dowry*, explains. Culture, background, family and previous sexual experience are just some of the factors which combine to produce a sexual legacy that influences our beliefs about sex and intimacy, as well as the way we behave and think. This can create misunderstanding and hurt if you each have different ways of expressing yourselves or different understandings about your behaviour. Ways to overcome this and to be more comfortable with your individual sexual styles is discussed in depth, along with some ideas about how to manage your feelings and behaviour when you encounter differences or misunderstandings.

How the uniqueness of the relationship combines with the sexual dramas we enact is considered in the final chapter of this section, *Sexual Performance*. If your relationship is relatively new, there is advice on how to combine the excitement, novelty and apprehension to make the early days of your relationship a solid base on which to build your sexual future and to identify and overcome early problems. There are some very practical ideas and exercises on how to create or rebuild a strong sensual and sexual relationship and how to overcome the anxiety associated with high personal expectations for sexual accomplishment or even just wanting to please your partner.

Part Three, **Overcoming Sexual Challenges**, provides the ideas you need to keep your relationship fresh in spite of the real-life pressures everyone encounters as life progresses. Whether the pressure is to do with finding time for yourselves as a couple amid the stresses of work, family and finance, or dismissing bad habits, there are plenty of realistic ideas about how to develop your relationship and sexual connection positively despite the pressures you are bound to experience.

The section begins with a look at *Body Knowledge* and how it affects feelings about yourself and your capacity to be sexually expressive. Both men and women experience concerns about the way they look and how that makes them feel, and our comfort with ourselves changes at different points in our lives. This section looks in particular at concerns about nudity and genital appearance. Reassuring explanation of how genitals look and function will help you to reacquaint yourself with your body.

The next chapter, about *Sexual Secrets*, discusses what happens when you discover something unknown about your partner's sexual behaviour, such as infidelity, cross-dressing, fetishes, internet pornography and cybersex. Even minor secrets may feel like an infidelity or betrayal, affecting your sense of yourself, as well as changing the way you see the relationship. Even when what you discover is something that can be embraced and incorporated into the relationship, adjustment can be challenging. Acknowledging that there is no helpful template for reactions in these circumstances, this chapter will discuss how to manage the situation, when outside help is necessary and how you can reunite sexually after the discovery of a sexual secret.

Ageing has a chapter to itself, as so many couples and individuals are concerned about the effects on sexuality of getting older – and often start worrying when they are very young. However, this chapter is not so much about growing old as managing the different stages of life as we pass through them and preparing ourselves to continue sexual activity throughout our lives. Expected changes to the body as we age are described, including the menopause, with detail about how to cope with them and when you may need help.

Ageing in itself need not be a barrier to sexual pleasure or enjoyment. It is the *Physical Limitations* associated with ageing which sometimes affect sexual functioning and are considered in the following chapter. This looks at practical ways to adapt when one or both of you are affected by chronic or limiting conditions, including information on sexual positions for comfort and pleasure. As well as including common conditions which are more obviously sexually related, such as those affecting reproduction, it will address familiar complaints which may make sex difficult, like a bad back, chronic fatigue and being overweight. Some of the more embarrassing problems – such as needing the loo during sex, poor hygiene and 'fanny farts' – are included too, always with an explanation of ways they may affect sex and ideas for management.

Then there is a crucial look at *Sexual Dysfunctions* – usually chronic sexual problems which get in the way of lovemaking. These include genital pain and difficulty with penetration, erectile disorders, problems with orgasm and persistent genital arousal. Each condition will be discussed in terms of its presentation, potential to treat and its effects on your relationship. As with the aspects of ageing and the physical limitations which are discussed in this section of the book, the overview of the condition should reassure you that what you are experiencing is not uncommon. This may also be helpful in understanding what your partner is going through, should they be affected. As each of the sexual dysfunctions and problems with desire can potentially be treated by *Psychosexual Therapy*, the final chapter in this section discusses what to expect from the psychosexual therapy process.

Part Four looks at ways of **Maintaining and Improving Your Sex Life**. It begins with a chapter on *Sexual Realism*, which is a reminder to work with your sexual relationship and sexual behaviour in accordance with what is possible. Management of ongoing desire issues, sexual frequency and how to make time for sex are among the topics included. Other challenges to intimacy which are tackled include lifestyle and associated behaviours, with their surprisingly potent effect on sex and intimacy. Times when sex is absent or rare are mentioned, along with some exercises to help if you wish to make changes.

Probably the most common reasons given by couples for coming to Relate concern communication problems, so the next chapter focuses on *Communicating* in relationships. It explores the way that sexual confidence ebbs and flows – and the reasons for this – and discusses why it is important to establish ways to deal with those times when either or both of you feel less sexy or are less easily aroused. There is also consideration of the ways your communication style can affect your ability to understand each other and develop a sexual language within your relationship, revisiting ways to avoid misunderstandings which threaten intimacy. There are exercises and advice on the development and maintenance of practical skills that will improve your communication and your confidence in communicating. This, in turn, could impact your sexual self-assurance and competence in a positive way.

Specific challenges to understanding are addressed, including the difficulties associated with Asperger syndrome, which can produce some particular obstacles to communication, as well as some sensory issues which can complicate relationships. The chapter concludes with practical advice on how to conduct a conversation effectively, whatever the topic.

Some sexual behaviours and ideas you may enjoy, or just be curious about, are explained in the chapter on *Safe Sexual Experimentation*. For instance, you may have heard about the G spot, but what do you know about the A spot or U spot? Have you come across tantric sex, frottage or edging? These and many other practices are explained, with ideas about how to incorporate them into your lovemaking if you wish to. Whether or not any of these are for you, this chapter aims to increase your comfort with your sexual pleasure and answer some of your questions. All the topics covered in this chapter have been brought to therapy for discussion by couples and are familiar to Relate's psychosexual therapists.

The conclusion, on *Celebrating Sexuality*, summarises some of the book's major points and encourages you to enjoy your sexual self and partnership. This last chapter is packed with advice about how to maintain your relationship intimacy and pleasure.

A Useful Reading list in the Resources section at the end of the book offers some suggestions of ways to obtain further information and explore topics in more detail.

The Relate Guide to Sex and Intimacy should have a permanent place on your bedside table, as it offers information and solutions to a vast range of issues affecting sex, intimacy and relationships, which may be experienced at different points in your life. Based on the extensive experience and skill Relate has developed over many years with thousands of people, it reflects the reality and challenges of modern relationships. As a Relate Institute lecturer and practising relationship and psychosexual therapist myself, I have made sure the book contains the information you need based on the questions, problems and successes of real-life 21st-century couples. I hope it can help to make the differences you desire.

Part One
Understanding Sex and Desire

Chapter One
Why Intimacy
Is Important

Allowing someone to get close to you is an achievement. You may want to be intimate, or try to avoid it, but when you find that special someone, you *know* – and your body knows. It's not just about goosebumps or tummy flips when that exceptional someone is near; it's about a gentler, longer-lasting sense of wellbeing that comes from knowing there is someone special in the world who thinks you're special too. This may not only be a lifelong connection; it may actually extend your life too.

SEX AND INTIMACY

One of the reasons sex and intimacy are great for your health and your relationship is that they provide an additional form of communication which is missing when you rely entirely on words. Non-verbal touch is sometimes necessary to support what we say or when we just don't have the words to express what we are feeling. Developing comfort with touching your partner helps you both to develop an additional language, which can be used whenever words are not enough. If you think back to your childhood, hugs rather than words were probably what you found most comforting, and the same is often true in our adult relationships as well.

Sexual touch

Ironically, though, the more you care about someone, the harder it can be to enjoy the relaxed sensuality of sexual touch, let alone to be experimental or daring. Even if you were once swinging from the chandeliers, carefree and sexually insatiable, you may find yourselves becoming far more sexually reticent once you really start to love each other. By then, sex really matters. With the acknowledgement of love comes an element of risk. Now you are sharing yourself, offering yourself and revealing yourself. The more in love you are, the more scared you may be of getting it wrong. For many couples, this is when sex can become less frequent or stop altogether, and then it may not be easy to begin again. New ways to communicate what is happening need to be found, including new ways to communicate sexually. This is when some couples seek psychosexual therapy, which deals specifically with sexual issues. It is explained in more detail in Chapter Twelve (see pages 182–90).

What is intimacy?

It can be difficult to define intimacy with a partner. In adults, the word 'intimacy' is often used as a euphemism for sex. However, though sex and intimacy feed each other, they don't always coexist. Though being sexual together improves feelings of intimacy, and intimacy can lead to being sexual, sex can feel anything but intimate if the circumstances aren't right. In fact, the reason loss of intimate feelings leads some people to avoid sex altogether is because it just reminds them of what they are missing.

Anything which affects just the two of you can feel intimate and special. But, more than that, partner intimacy probably gives you a feeling of belonging. You feel safe, you have someone you trust on your side, you can be vulnerable without feeling judged. This allows you to be sexual together in a way which takes into account the special feelings you have for one another. This extraordinary relationship lets you be yourself, knowing that even when you get it wrong with each other, or don't agree, there are enough shared experiences and enough willingness to support each other to be sure you can get through anything.

If that all sounds too good to be true it is because there is so much in life which can intrude on relationships and impair intimacy. You may even feel that you can seldom or never relax enough together. If only you just had each other to think about you might never become irritable or moody, feel rejected or misunderstood. However, as well as starting to worry about how we nurture the relationship once we feel it is serious and lasting, all the other responsibilities in our lives – such as children and work – can easily get in the way of intimacy and it can all seem too much.

Yet sex and intimacy in your relationship are definitely worth striving for, however hard it may be. The benefits are not only those feelings of satisfaction, wellbeing and comfort derived from a physically close relationship. For a start, if you feel good about yourself, it shows. Other people like what they see and this may allow you to be more relaxed and to make the most of all your relationships; even your work or study may benefit. Your children will certainly profit from seeing their parents engaged and cooperating, as well as from the good mood and tolerance that is engendered by a satisfying sex life and supportive intimacy.

Better health

There is also considerable evidence that intimate relationships are very good for our physical and mental health. Both are thought to be improved when sex and intimacy are part of our lives. Sex is good mild exercise, which raises the heart rate, and this may help to lower blood pressure and improve overall cardiovascular fitness. Sex may also reduce headaches, prevent stomach ulcers in men and osteoporosis in women, help with insomnia and ease tension and stress. Moreover, it may improve memory and reduce the risk of dementia and infections. Indeed, sexually active people have been shown to have significantly higher levels of the antibody immunoglobulin A and hormones which both reduce inflammation and promote healing.

Arousal and orgasm are thought to ease pain and have been shown to be particularly effective in helping to treat menstrual cramps. Clitoral stimulation can offer some pain relief in childbirth and can also accelerate labour. In women, the increased levels of oestrogen associated with sex may offer protection against heart disease, while regular ejaculation in men is thought to lower the risk of developing prostate cancer.

Hormones released during arousal and orgasm can even make you look younger, as collagen production is stimulated, which creates smoother-looking, more supple skin. There is also no doubt that sex is a great reliever of tension, associated with reduction of the stress hormone cortisol and increased levels of pleasure-promoting hormones. Even just hugging is believed to reduce stress. People who are less tense and stressed, and who enjoy regular intimacy, tend to feel more confident and relaxed, which probably also helps improve their appearance and boost immune responses.

So why are many people still not as comfortable as they would like to be with their sexual expression and intimacy?

Though masturbation and casual sex both contribute somewhat to these positive health effects, enjoyable sex teamed with intimacy is significantly good for us. However, it is not as simple as finding a partner and getting physical to reap relationship rewards. The way the relationship works, our attitudes and beliefs, our ability to share and relax and our wish to be sexual all contribute to the way we 'do' relationships and how much they help us. There are so many things that can make us want sex or turn us off it, and just as many that make us satisfied with our relationships and sex lives, it is no wonder that at any time about half of us are feeling a bit disappointed.

The idea that other people are having a better time or are more sexually skilled than we are contributes to feelings of dissatisfaction. We may form this impression from what other people tell us or, more likely, from the impression given on television, in social media, films, magazines and newspapers. The huge changes in society during the past few decades have improved our access to information about sex and relationships and have made sexual expression and diversity something to celebrate rather than be ashamed of. This means we are seeing and hearing much more about sex than was ever previously likely or possible. While increased openness is a positive move forward, this also places more demands on couples to aspire to an ideal of 'good', 'satisfying' sex and for couples to believe they are alone if they don't feel 100 per cent happy with their sex lives.

The media is bursting with images of romance and sexual longing. Many of these suggest that sex needs to be unusual in some way, if only to prevent sexual boredom. It has made us much more likely to put pressure on ourselves to have not just satisfying sexual experiences, but to seek utterly mind-blowing sexual encounters. The invisible coercion all around us causes worry that our sex life could be considered boring even when we are enjoying it. This means that much of the concern about sex is around people's expectations of what they *ought* to be doing, not what they actually *enjoy* doing. This creates artificial demands which are constraining in themselves.

When all is not as we expect it ought to be, we often medicalise what we see as the problem; that is, we sometimes assume it is entirely a physical issue which can be resolved medically. Of course, this creates even more concern if medicine doesn't come up with a solution. Don't misunderstand; it is incredibly important to get medical checks for physical problems. However, the vast majority of sexual concerns – whether they have a physical origin or not – are made much worse by the way we think.

*

Try the exercise below on holding hands to see how it makes you feel to touch each other with no sexual agenda at all, but with lots of interest and care. It may feel silly at first but that doesn't matter. After all, laughing together can only bring you closer. This exercise isn't meant to be compared with sex, just enjoyed as a stand-alone experiment to see how comfortable you are with touch and closeness. If you find it really difficult and just want to get down to some sexual action, think about all the sensual and erotic possibilities you could be missing out on.

EXERCISE: HOLDING HANDS

➤ Sit or lie opposite your partner.

➤ When you are comfortable, take both of their hands in yours.

➤ Examine the hands all over, back and front. Take your time, turning them over, weighing them in your hands and exploring them from the tips of the fingers to the wrists.

➤ Gently rest one hand and now pay attention to the other, inspecting each finger in turn. Look in between them, touch them with your own fingertips and also pay attention to the palm, back of the hand, nails and wrist. Kiss, nuzzle or lick each finger if you want to. What do you notice? Is the hand rough or smooth? Is it hairy? Are the nails short or long? Does the colour vary? Are there spots or rough areas?

➤ Finally, cup the hand between your own hands and hold it to you before resting it.

➤ Then turn your attention to the other hand and repeat the previous two steps. Notice whether it is easier the second time. If you feel the first hand missed out, return to it and give it the attention you now feel it deserves.

➤ When you have finished, take both hands again and guide them to touch your arms, shoulders and head.

➤ Only when you feel your examination is truly over should you swap and allow your partner to examine your hands.

➤ When you have each finished your turn, hold each other's heads gently and spend a few moments caressing them while gazing into each other's eyes.

If you find non-sexual touching very difficult, you may believe that any sexual feeling – be it a thought or physical arousal – should be acted on. Perhaps you even believe you will be ill if you don't use your erection or if you ignore your arousal. The reality, though, is that ignoring arousal won't affect your health. It is rare in real life for two people to have sexual feelings at exactly the same time. Even on, say, a romantic evening when you are both expecting sex, mutual desire can't always be relied on. Indeed, it is extremely likely and common that sometimes one or both of you probably goes along with sex, hoping to become aroused, but without the initial desire.

If this exercise doesn't seem to go far enough, or if you enjoyed it and want more, there is more guidance on non-sexual touching on page 85, or you could just experiment. Sensual touch can be a delicious alternative to active sex, a great end to a stressful day and a terrific way to begin or end lovemaking. Couples often like to give one another a massage, which can be very pleasant but is very different from sensual touch. Barely touching at all can set the nerves tingling. You can use your fingertips, feathers, lips, hair or you can even blow gently across the skin. This is a completely different experience depending on which part of the body you choose. Don't worry if it tickles to begin with. If you fall around laughing, so what? Since when did sex and sensuality have to be deadly serious?

SEXUAL BEHAVIOURS

Though intercourse is often valued much more highly than other forms of sexual expression, these may enhance the overall experience of a sexual encounter which ends with intercourse or may be satisfying on their own, either some of the time or always.

Sexual problems usually arise not because of what you do together or want, but because of what you *think* you should be doing or think everyone else is doing. Look at the list below and see how many of these sexual behaviours you participate in and then compare this with how many you *could* participate in. Think about what stops you.

- Taking pleasure in fixing hair or make-up
- Wearing clothes that make you feel good
- Looking at yourself in the mirror clothed
- Looking at yourself in the mirror naked
- Exploring your own body
- Flirting
- Touching as you pass each other
- Phoning or texting your partner
- Leaving messages or notes for your partner
- Hugging your partner
- Looking into each other's eyes
- Holding hands
- Dancing on your own
- Dancing as a couple
- Catching your partner's eye in a crowd
- Snuggling together on the sofa

- Spending a morning in bed together
- Deep kissing
- Touching one another while clothed
- Lying together naked
- Giving/receiving massage
- Washing or brushing each other's hair
- Showering or bathing together
- Whispering sexual promises or wishes
- Sensual or arousing touch and caressing
- Oral sex
- Intercourse

You could probably go on and on adding to this list as you realise all the things that make you feel sexy. Notice that not all behaviours in the list are about sex with your partner – or about having sex at all in some cases. If you think of sex as only intercourse, then it may be difficult to 'have sex' as often as you would like to, particularly when tiredness, your hectic life and lack of opportunity get in the way.

If you did only one item from the list each day, you would still be including sexuality in your life. Most of us do many more than one without even noticing. Whether or not you are satisfied with your sex life as it is, there is no harm in seeing if there is more you could include from the list and probably quite a bit more you could add to it. Enjoying little episodes of arousal could become part of your day if you let them.

Gay couples seem to have fewer reported sexual problems than straight couples. Some gay readers may be thinking that much of this can be put down to the fact that they are more accepting of sexual activities which don't include intercourse. Though intercourse may be a part of your sexual repertoire if you are a gay man or woman, you may also be more creative and more aware of sexual opportunities than some straight couples and even better able to communicate your sexual interests. There may also be a gender bias about how sexual communication develops. You may be aware of this in your own relationship, whether you are gay or straight. The expectations about how each gender ought to behave undoubtedly influence our thinking and behaviour, as the next chapter demonstrates.

Chapter Two
Gender Differences

The way we think about gender probably includes some stereotypes which focus on differences rather than similarities. For instance, different behaviours are associated with different gender character-istics. Caring or fussy behaviour may be seen as feminine while aggressive or uncaring behaviour is considered masculine. As a result, some women feel guilty if they behave assertively and some men feel they will be criticised for being too soft. In reality, basic feelings of wanting to be close and cared for apply equally to men and women, but the way we show and manage our feelings may be different.

Some stereotypes about gender differences in relation to sex are helpful, but many are not. For instance, a stereotypical view of women is that they are less interested in sex than men, more likely to see sex as indicating commitment, less spontaneous, more difficult to arouse, less likely to initiate sex and less sexually adventurous than men. Equally, a view of men is that they are only interested in sex, averse to commitment but always ready for intercourse. Some of this may be true for some people some of the time, but it sounds like an awful lot of pressure and certainly doesn't apply to everyone.

SEX AS A RELATIONSHIP BAROMETER

In women there does, however, seem to be a circular association between overall wellbeing and sexual contentment. It is hardly surprising to learn that these contribute to one another. By no means all, but many men believe that a sexual encounter will cure both general and relationship problems, whereas women are more likely to need their relationship to be okay before they want to behave sexually. Also, men are likely to see sexual frequency as a relationship barometer, indicating how well things are going, while women are more likely to value talking as a sign that the relationship is going well. In other words, men's idea that intercourse indicates that the relationship is blossoming may motivate them to seek sex more often. Thus, sex is not just reassuring and comforting in itself; the act can be seen as having meaning about you as a couple.

It is easy to see how this difference could be construed as a high sex drive in the man when, in fact, the woman's desire for a sexual experience may actually be equal or greater. His desire may be not so much about a yearning for sex as a need to have evidence of intimacy and confirmation of the strength of the relationship through sex. Both men and women who need this sort of affirmation probably won't be consciously thinking very much about this or why they want sex – they just do and it feels very important to them.

On the surface, then, men may have fewer episodes of felt emotional intimacy but more episodes of 'sexual desire' than women do. There are also some theories that men are less prepared to take emotional risks than women and therefore avoid becoming as close as women do. The risk of rejection by their primary partner has even been argued to account for some men's serial affairs.

Though feelings of intimacy do clearly go hand in hand with sexual satisfaction and contentment, all this suggests that reassurance can be a significant reason for seeking sex and may be necessary before intimacy can be properly experienced, regardless of gender. Because this need presents itself in different ways, whether you are in a straight, gay or trans relationship, these differences often translate into the idea that one of the couple is highly sexed and the other is lacking in desire.

SEXUAL FREQUENCY

It is hardly worth saying that this is all relative. Sexual encounters twice a day would be average for some couples while others would be pleased to be sexual twice a year and some are perfectly satisfied with no sex at all. Often, both people in a couple are actually satisfied with their level of intimacy and sexual frequency, but feel they *ought* to be sexual more often. Frequency is only a problem when one or both of you see it as a problem.

It is common for one partner to appear to want more sex than the other, but uncommon for couples to discuss this. Instead, they often develop behaviours which seek or avoid sex, usually making them thoroughly miserable and damaging their overall chances of intimacy. A ridiculously simple solution is just to discuss how to manage this. It may be that you need to negotiate how much physical contact is reasonable given your circumstances – how tired, stressed and busy you are, for instance. The danger is that all physical contact comes to be seen as a prelude to sex. Clearly agreed boundaries around this help prevent a pleasant kiss and cuddle turning into a battle. Choosing an appropriate moment to make sexual approaches is also crucial; the end of a long and tiring day may not be the best time. Indeed, finding the most appropriate times for sex may take planning. *Without* discussion and planning, sexual frequency can start to be used as evidence of each partner's lack of understanding rather than a perfectly reasonable wish to be close or to decline sex.

Nonetheless, the idea that one partner has a high sex drive and the other has a low one, or has 'gone off it', may feel less blaming and hurtful to each partner than the thought that they might be deliberately withholding sex or demanding it for selfish reasons. It would be much more useful, though, to just talk about it and ensure that some level of physical intimacy and interest is maintained even if it is difficult to fit in intercourse very often.

Think carefully about what stops you from negotiating sexual frequency. One reason why so many couples persist with the idea that they have different sex drives, rather than discussing the issue in more depth, may be that it doesn't just remove blame, it takes away responsibility, suggesting that we are all at the mercy of our genetic make-up. That's okay as far as it goes, but thinking this way also eliminates the possibility of change or choice. For instance, if you tell yourself you ought to have intercourse whenever your partner wants you to, you are likely to grow resentful towards your partner if they want to make love more than you do. You may also be cross with yourself for not complying – though you may not be entirely clear why. This uncomfortable feeling can stop you from starting a discussion, especially if you are not entirely sure where you want to go with it. However, no one has to have sex just because their partner wants to. Sometimes a warm kiss and cuddle can be just as satisfying – pestering for sex or rejecting it, however, are hurtful and end up damaging your feelings about each other.

You also don't need to feel guilty because you don't want the same things. There are always alternative ways of thinking and behaving that don't fill you with shame or a need to blame someone else.

You may be thinking that your partner's approaches are all about the pleasure involved in the sexual act rather than lovemaking, but there are probably times when you too just want sex. The pleasure doesn't switch off your love; it might even enhance it. So why do you only notice your partner's desire to have sex rather than the desire to have sex with *you*? You probably feel that, by pestering you for sex, your partner is ignoring how tired and busy you are and only thinking about their own needs. Meanwhile, your partner may be thinking that you are rejecting them because you don't find them attractive or because you are trying to punish them. As a result, they may feel it is more important than ever to have sex to prove the relationship is okay. They may even feel ashamed that you aren't as interested as they are and blame you so that they can keep their shame at bay.

See what's happened? Both your insecurities are playing a major role in your attitude to lovemaking. The joy of intimacy and the sheer fun of relaxed sex have vanished. Sex has become all about point scoring and avoiding feeling bad, rather than making yourself and each other feel good. That's not what you intended, I'll bet.

CHANGE YOUR SEXUAL THINKING

Try thinking that sexual needs don't really exist – but that emotional needs do. If you see your partner's constant wish for sex as a need for reassurance, rather than just a biological itch, you may feel more able to offer reassurance in other areas too. This could prove extraordinarily helpful if you have become irritable about what you see as sexual pestering and responded by pushing your partner away, which probably only increases the pestering anyway. Similarly, if you recognise that emotional needs are the ones your partner is paying most attention to, you will also become aware that your constant pestering isn't going to persuade them to leap into bed with you. They may, however, respond to more romantic overtures and expressions of your care.

The points below offer some simple ideas about how to start thinking in ways that will remove some of the pressure you both may be feeling, improve the lovemaking experience for you and your partner, make you feel more sexual generally and probably lead to improved communication about sex. In trying to think differently about sex with your partner, remember the following:

- Don't be hung up on intercourse.
- Try not to blame yourself or your partner.

- Avoid making assumptions; check out what your partner is *actually* thinking rather than just accepting what you suppose.
- Recognise when you are feeling and being sexual.
- Appreciate when your partner is offering affection and intimacy.
- Assess what is possible.
- Stop worrying.

SEXUAL TRIGGERS

Practically anything could trigger desire for sex, as this is very personal. This could be an arousing picture, an attractive partner, a need for stress relief, success for your football team, a feeling of entitlement or a sense of closeness and love. Sometimes there is no trigger but you may feel you ought to feel desire and take your cue. For instance, this may happen when you are on holiday or when your partner has made a special effort. Men are more likely than women to respond to what they perceive as sexual triggers. This doesn't, however, mean that all men are always ready for sex; they are just as likely to be distracted or tired as women. However, triggers for women are sometimes subtler and more related to feelings of intimacy. Often, desire for sexual behaviour *follows* arousal rather than the other way round. Because this means women can sometimes be persuaded to join in with sex when they have said they aren't in the mood, it is understandable that partners persist in trying. However, even when they do feel aroused, some women will refuse to engage because they feel hurt or angry. They are less likely than men to believe that sex will fix everything. Couples often present for sex therapy with very different ideas about motivation for lovemaking, one partner hoping it will make things better and the other feeling that to 'give in' will equal humiliation and communicate unwarranted forgiveness. This is very difficult to negotiate when women are notoriously interested in intimacy and men are notoriously interested in creating intimacy through intercourse. Saying you want the intimacy before you'll have sex is just plain baffling for some men.

Avoiding a knee-jerk reaction to sexual approaches will improve your chances of changing how you conduct your relationship. The earlier section about changing your thinking (see page 24) contains ideas about alternative ways to approach old habits. Thinking about what you actually want, and why you want it, is more helpful than pursuing demands or avoiding them on a point of principle. Chapter Fourteen, on communication, offers ways to approach contentious issues like this in a non-threatening way. The trouble is that you may be concentrating on the effect on yourself rather than thinking about how your partner feels. Showing some understanding of this is more likely to make them interested in how you feel than if you constantly just repeat your take on the situation.

Sometimes, it is possible to plan different behaviour. Women see their desire as fluctuating at different points in their menstrual cycle and at different times in their life, and knowing this can help you both to manage the high and low points.

Desire is likely to be most noticeable for women in the middle of the month when they ovulate and their chance of pregnancy is high, but situations and emotional influences can be even more significant in determining whether a woman wants to behave sexually. Women also respond differently to men to different stimuli. For instance, if a straight couple were to see a film of another couple making love, the man would most likely be aroused in an observer role, watching the act. Meanwhile, the woman's process would be more likely to involve identifying with the woman in the film and emotionally putting herself in the story. This isn't happening consciously, but it may explain why women can take slightly longer to engage with sexual ideas and do so in a more roundabout way than men.

Responsive versus active desire

It is commonly believed that women are more 'responsive' in their desire, which means they need encouragement to feel it. Meanwhile, men are expected to be more 'active' and as a result more likely to take the initiative sexually. Nevertheless, there are many men who also rarely experience 'desire' but enjoy sex when they participate. This can be a problem if both partners wait for the other to initiate sex or when a partner believes men should 'always be up for it'. On the other hand, partners may appreciate the opportunity to initiate sexual encounters more often themselves. Some people find it extremely arousing for their partner to control their sexual experiences and much prefer to take a passive role. However, when partners are subtle about their sexual cues, what they think indicates a desire to be sexual may not always be picked up, especially if that is the last thing on the other's mind at the time. This can lead to distress and feelings of rejection.

For instance, Jaz was fuming and hurt when Ash went straight to the study to work after a candlelit dinner. He didn't share Jaz's understanding that lighting candles at dinner time was a romantic clue and was preoccupied with work in any case. Similarly, Coleen felt humiliated when Paul continued getting ready to go out for the evening without apparently noticing that she was walking around their bedroom naked. Assuming she was undressed because she couldn't decide what to wear, Paul was flabbergasted when Coleen later complained that he had rejected her sexual advances.

Complete the quiz on sexual desire to see if your desire is active or responsive. The results will help you to understand your own sexual feelings and why you may not feel desire when your partner expects you to. Sharing this information with your partner may relieve some of the pressure you may feel to experience desire – or not to.

QUIZ: IS YOUR SEXUAL DESIRE RESPONSIVE OR ACTIVE?

1. Do you look forward to sex?
    - a) Most of the time
    - b) Sometimes
    - c) Rarely or never

2. Are you usually the one to initiate sex?
    - a) Almost always
    - b) Sometimes
    - c) Rarely or never

3. Do you avoid cuddles in case they lead to sex?
    - a) Rarely or never
    - b) Sometimes
    - c) Almost always

4. Do you often feel aroused thinking about your partner?
    - a) Almost always
    - b) Sometimes
    - c) Rarely or never

5. Do you often have sex when you don't really want to?
    - a) Rarely or never
    - b) Sometimes
    - c) Almost always

6. Do you find you often only become aroused once you start having sex?
    - a) Rarely or never
    - b) Sometimes
    - c) Almost always

Mostly As

You most likely have an active approach to sex. You think about it a lot and are often on the lookout for sexual opportunities.

Mostly Bs

The way you respond is probably affected by your circumstances and how able you are to relax rather than any innate desire tendency.

Mostly Cs

You seem to have a responsive approach to sex. You don't think about it that much, but you enjoy it once you get going.

It doesn't help to think that your partner should 'fix' your sexual frustration or that you have a duty to 'fix' theirs. This attitude leads to resentment and a vicious cycle of sexual pursuit and distancing. It is more helpful to take responsibility for your own sexual needs and determine which of your feelings are caused by sexual frustration and which are more about relationship concerns or lack of closeness.

If both of you have a responsive desire pattern, you could choose to schedule sensual and sexual time for occasions when you are both able to relax and devote yourselves to the experience. Finding those times isn't necessarily easy, especially if you think of them as involving effort. Taking the pressure off by thinking that they are times to be close and have a kiss and cuddle, rather than 'have sex', means you can enjoy the sensuality and closeness this involves and just see where it leads. Similarly, if one of you has more active desire, it is worth planning for times when your partner is most likely to be relaxed and unstressed in order to maximise interest. As suggested above, around ovulation in the middle of the menstrual cycle is when women are most likely to experience spontaneous desire, but both of you may need to pay attention to this to find out what works for you. Again, if you are an active–responsive couple, making scheduled intimate experiences about intimacy and sensuality may or may not lead on to sex but, at the very least, you will feel close. If you are less active, don't be afraid to show affection in case your partner thinks you want sex. Improving the bond between you by being affectionate makes it easier to negotiate how you manage the differences in your desire.

One reason that couples find themselves having problems with different levels of desire is how it makes them feel about themselves. For instance, it may be hurtful to feel that your partner wants sex rather than to make love or you may feel your partner's lack of desire means you aren't a 'good enough' man or woman. Sexual frequency and your partner's interest can bolster your feelings of sexual wellbeing and adequacy. This is explored in the next chapter, which looks at your sexual image.

Chapter Three
Your Sexual Image

Even if you don't much care what other people think, you probably have an image of yourself, or an image you aspire to, which is demonstrated by all the things you say and do. Though this may give others a message about what to expect from you, it also has an important role in your own sense of ease with yourself. We all have aspects of our lives and things we do that we feel proud or ashamed of. We like it when we do things which make us feel proud of the way we are, or at least comfortable with ourselves. Our sexual image is a big part of this. Even though much of what contributes to this is very private, we still care what it says about us.

For you to feel relaxed with your sexuality, your sexual self needs to be someone you are aware of, value and can comfortably express. You may think there is a time and place for sexual expression. You would be right; it is probably best not to start snogging your partner during parents' evening at school or while sitting in a church pew during a funeral. However, though you may choose not to behave sexually on these occasions, you may still be sexually aware. Indeed, choosing *not* to behave sexually, if you would like to, demonstrates your sexual awareness.

You may be aware that you have taken trouble over your appearance, that you smell good, that your skin feels fresh and soft and that your overall appearance is attractive. This is more of a sensual awareness, but it still contributes to your self as a sexual being. There are more obvious sexual moments. You may catch your partner's eye, touch ever so softly and briefly as your hands brush together, enjoy a stolen kiss, make a flirty comment or simply look in the mirror and think you look great. These are all expressions of your sexuality that have no sexual act involved, but they can contribute to feelings of intimacy, desire and arousal, as well as your overall sense of wellbeing and satisfaction. However, though sex and sexuality are a 'natural' part of our make-up, we spend a lot of time ignoring our sensual and sexual selves or even repressing feelings associated with ourselves as sexual.

EXERCISE: BECOMING SEXUALLY AWARE

The questions below about becoming sexually aware offer considerable insight into the way you are now as well as how you got there. There are no right or wrong answers, but they should provoke lots of food for thought – just for you or for your partner too if you discuss your answers.

➤ When was the first time you felt aroused? What caused this?
➤ Do you enjoy making yourself look good?
➤ Does feeling attractive affect your confidence generally?
➤ Were you surprised by who you found yourself attracted to?
➤ Did you have any crushes?
➤ How did your first sexual experience with another person come about? Was it pleasant or disappointing?
➤ How did it make you feel about yourself?
➤ Were you orgasmic?

➤ What about first intercourse?

➤ Was it how you imagined it would be?

➤ Were you enthusiastic? Wary? Coerced?

➤ What were the circumstances? Was the situation romantic? Sordid? Unexpected?

➤ How did it affect the way you thought of yourself?

➤ Did it affect your subsequent sexual behaviour?

➤ How comfortable do you feel with nudity?

➤ Do you feel able to be vulnerable with your partner?

➤ Do you feel comfortable initiating sex?

➤ Do you enjoy feeling aroused or push down feelings of arousal?

➤ Do you feel comfortable with your sexuality?

➤ Do you feel like a healthy sexual being?

Questions like these are often very helpful in showing you why you feel or think the way you do. There may be aspects you have never considered before or you may have thought about these ideas a great deal. You may even find that your attitude and answers to the questions vary from day to day depending on your mood and what else is going on. For instance, you may answer that you feel uncomfortable with nudity on a day when you have a cold, a period, you feel fat or work was difficult. However, you may say you do feel comfortable with nudity on a day when you have slept well, feel you look good, things went well at work and you are feeling close to your partner. In other words, your mood, the context, your health, how others are behaving and your life at the time all contribute to how able you are to pay attention to expressing your sexuality or being intimate. Though it may be a high priority to you to nurture the relationship with your partner, you just may not have the time as your days become eaten up with trying to juggle all your responsibilities at once.

SEX IS NATURAL – ISN'T IT?

The word 'natural' is often associated with sex. People say that it is *natural* to want sex, have sex and be sexual. The idea of sex as a natural act can lead us to believe that it *ought* to be easy and problem-free. Ideas about what easy means lead to beliefs that couples should climax simultaneously or that women should always orgasm during intercourse, both of which are actually rare occurrences which look good in movies and read well in books. Perfect encounters where couples are aroused at the twang of knicker elastic – and proceed swiftly to mind-blowing multiple orgasms together – don't portray the fumbling, the rummaging for a condom, the time it can take to get wet enough for penetration, the need for lube, the niggling thought that you should really have had an early night, the preoccupation with disguising your tubby tummy, pins and needles in your arm, the need for a shower first, the wet patch afterwards. These are all normal, everyday occurrences – if you don't recognise any of them, you are very, very lucky and very unusual. The jokes comedians make about sexual slip-ups wouldn't be funny if we didn't have an expectation that something else would happen, that there is a way of getting our sex lives perfectly right. The jokes subtly tell us what normal and natural should be and we may laugh at what goes wrong in relief as much as amusement.

Because we are brought up with romantic notions of sex, we inevitably develop unrealistic expectations of what it involves. Many people's early sexual experiences aren't quite what they imagined or hoped for. This may just be chalked up to lack of experience, but it can plant the idea that you are doing something wrong.

First sexual experiences

Early non-penetrative sexual experiences may or may not lead to orgasm but may be very satisfying for both partners. The newness of it all contributes to the pleasure. When intercourse is attempted, however, the equivalent pleasure may not result. The same attention may not be paid to touch, with both partners in a hurry to get to intercourse. Straight couples often assume the woman will climax through vaginal penetration. In the event, it may all be over surprisingly quickly, perhaps before penetration even occurs. Penetration may be difficult and even painful, especially if the woman is anxious. It may be hard to talk about what happened, especially if the partners are worried they did something wrong or don't want to admit they are disappointed.

Some early same-sex sexual encounters may be more open than straight ones. This could be when the couple doesn't have the same unrealistic romantic expectation and pressure to perform. For straight couples, there are added concerns about pregnancy and contraception, and for all couples there is worry about sexually transmitted diseases and fears about performance. Those early sexual experiences can then be remembered as much more satisfying and light-hearted. But, for many, there is no going back after intercourse. From now on, this will be 'real', grown-up sex.

Though by no means all early sexual experiences go wrong when the decision is made to start having intercourse, the combination of sexual inexperience and shyness can make communicating about what is happening really difficult. This may be more likely if you want your partner to do something differently or fear that you are doing something wrong. For many people it feels much easier to say nothing and hope for the best than to talk about it and risk being ridiculed. This, in itself, can affect the way you feel about your body and your sexual image. It can then be very easy to lose touch with what influences and motivates your feelings about yourself and the way your sexuality is expressed.

EXERCISE: YOUR SEXUAL BEGINNINGS

Answering the questions below will help to show what may have led to your current way of thinking about sex and your ability to be sexual, leading to the way you think about your body and your sexual image.

➤ When did you become aware of your body as a source of pleasure?
➤ Were you always comfortable touching your own body?
➤ Did anyone ever stop you from touching yourself?
➤ If so, how was this done and how did it make you feel?
➤ When and how did you become aware of sex?
➤ Who was most helpful in your learning about sex?
➤ Who has been least helpful?
➤ Was affectionate touch part of your everyday life as a child – did your family hug, kiss and express warmth and care in physical ways?
➤ Were you ever inappropriately touched? If so, did you ever tell anyone and what was the response?
➤ When did you discover masturbation?
➤ Did masturbating make you feel great or ashamed?
➤ Are there religious or cultural prohibitions on touch which influence the way you think?
➤ How did you feel about your first menstruation/ejaculation?
➤ Were you prepared for this? If so, by whom and how was it handled?
➤ Did you tell anyone about it?
➤ Again, what was the response? How did it affect your self-image?

> ➤ When did you start to feel you could express yourself
> sexually?
> ➤ What has changed since then?

It is unlikely that consideration of these questions will elicit no response at all. Thinking about some of these ideas may stir up concerns that perhaps have been buried or they may make you feel very positive about your sexual development. Either way, talking to your partner about what you have been thinking can be helpful, or you could discuss the questions together in the first place. They are likely to give you a much better idea of the way you each think and feel and how you came to be that way. Because our body and sexual images contribute so much to our view of ourselves, they are tied in with past experiences and our hopes for the way others see us.

Of course, some experiences we have make a negative contribution to self-image and may even make it more difficult to trust others, including partners. It is these aspects of your life or upbringing that you may find it hard to talk about. If you find it really difficult and need some help with this, these are the kind of areas which relationship therapists are well used to discussing. On the other hand, some people find they want to ask their parents or siblings more questions about their lives and enjoy the sense of discovery this brings about.

UNDERSTANDING YOUR SEXUAL SELF

Some people cope by avoiding thinking about their bodies and sexuality. So you may think that you don't have a sexual image, but we all do. Whether you are consciously aware of it or not, we have many images of ourselves that we check all the time. For instance, you may have ideas about what makes you feel like a parent, a sibling, a friend, a lover or that just contribute to your overall sense of yourself. There are things you do which say 'I am the kind of person who …' Each of these aspects of yourself probably has a story or background which contributes to your sense of who you are. For instance, when you are driving you may have a pleasant sense that you are the kind of person who drives a smart car or a fast car or an environmentally friendly car. This says something about you and there will be a story which explains why you like that image. For instance, Kap always wanted a smart car because all the men in his family drove them. They told him that if he worked hard at school, he would be able to afford a car like that. So, for Kap, a smart car equals not only evidence of his success but also says he is a hard worker who, presumably, deserves that success.

We all have similar stories and beliefs about our sexual selves even if we aren't fully aware of them. Try the exercise below on your sexual self and think about the stories which have contributed to that way of seeing yourself. There are no right or wrong statements, but they build a picture of how you show and feel your sexuality.

EXERCISE: BUILDING OURSELVES
Tick the statements that apply to you.

➤ I am the kind of person who enjoys physical touch.
➤ I am the kind of person who is embarrassed by physical touch.
➤ I am the kind of person who enjoys making the most of my appearance.
➤ I am the kind of person who dresses to fade into the background.

➤ I am the kind of person who is delighted by unexpected feelings of arousal.

➤ I am the kind of person who tries to push down unexpected feelings of arousal.

➤ I am the kind of person who never has unexpected feelings of arousal.

➤ I am the kind of person who loves attention.

➤ I am the kind of person who dislikes attention.

➤ I am the kind of person who sometimes shows off to encourage positive comments about my appearance.

➤ I am the kind of person who loves flirting.

➤ I am the kind of person who sometimes flirts.

➤ I am the kind of person who only flirts with my partner.

➤ I am the kind of person who never flirts.

➤ I am the kind of person who enjoys sending/receiving intimate texts.

➤ I am the kind of person who likes dancing.

➤ I am the kind of person who particularly likes dancing with a partner.

➤ I am the kind of person who doesn't like dancing.

➤ I am the kind of person who feels comfortable being sexual with my partner.

➤ I am the kind of person who sometimes feels awkward being sexual with my partner.

➤ I am the kind of person who enjoys sexual foreplay.

➤ I am the kind of person who prefers intercourse to foreplay.

➤ I am the kind of person who likes a slow burn before a sexual encounter.

➤ I am the kind of person who likes to get on with intercourse.

➤ I am the kind of person who enjoys compliments.

➤ I am the kind of person who is embarrassed by compliments.

➤ I am the kind of person who spends time in the bath or shower.

➤ I am the kind of person who washes quickly and efficiently.

➤ I am the kind of person who hates being naked.

➤ I am the kind of person who enjoys being naked.

➤ I am the kind of person who feels comfortable with my sexuality.

➤ I am the kind of person who feels uncomfortable with my sexuality.

➤ I am the kind of person who can initiate sex when I want to.

➤ I am the kind of person who would like to be more sexually expressive.

➤ I am the kind of person who feels comfortable with my sexual expression.

Some of the personal stories which have led to these beliefs may be strongly influenced by the views of others around you or by what you believe being sexual says about you. Are they worn-out stories which you could replace with a new way of thinking or are they still relevant and appropriate to the person you are or would like to become? Recognising the stories that underpin the statements will help you to work out whether there is anything you would like to change. It may also make you more aware of circumstances when you feel sexual. For example, getting ready for a night out often kick-starts feelings of sensuality and, perhaps, the idea of sexual expression.

Indeed, when you are taking a long bath, really revelling in the warm water and the lovely smells, when you are getting dressed, looking in the mirror and looking forward to a great night – it's then that you are aware of your sexual self; it's then that you can really start to strut your stuff.

Interestingly, you may ultimately feel more affirmed, and even admired, by others when you are comfortable with your own image. We can learn a lot from each other – the people who are most relaxed about developing their sexual selves and expressing their sexuality may not be those you would automatically assume to have the greatest sexual confidence. We are all aware of some people who are able to turn traditionally unattractive characteristics into an advantage or carry them off with such aplomb that you can't imagine them any other way. Rather than avoiding thinking about what they don't like in themselves or aren't sure of, they confront their doubts and dislikes head on, becoming so familiar with them that they can manage their uncertainty. Doing this opens our eyes to the way other people are feeling too, so we aren't so wrapped up in what's wrong with us that we don't realise how uncertain others are. Knowing you aren't alone does wonders for all aspects of your confidence – sexual confidence in particular.

ENJOYING AROUSAL

It can become a habit to push away sexual feelings in a manner that becomes automatic. This can start because we gather in childhood or adolescence that to feel sexual is wrong and this can be a difficult feeling to shake off. Sometimes, though, we repress our sexual feelings because we feel aroused in situations which are inappropriate. Our fight and flight responses can sometimes make us feel aroused when we are threatened, for instance. At other times, we may become aroused for no apparent reason but feel we haven't time for it, that our partners won't respond or that it is bad for our health not to act on feelings of arousal. This doesn't really deal with the issue at all but it does affect the way sexual image develops. If you are constantly pushing sexual feelings away, you are not only neglecting your sexual image but inadvertently developing a sexual persona which has difficulty with itself. You create a role for yourself in which you are avoiding sex and intimacy rather than embracing them because you see them as troublesome. If and when you then do want to be sexual, you struggle to know how to go about it; it doesn't come naturally as your instinct is to reject sexual feelings. This way of approaching their sexuality affects many people who see the whole issue of *how* they are sexual as hugely problematic.

There is no reason why you can't enjoy arousal, wherever it happens. Remembering your sexual encounter of last night as you travel to work may be extremely pleasurable, for example. Indulging your sexual memories and fantasies, and allowing yourself to become aroused, releases healthy endorphins which are good for cardiovascular and mental wellbeing.

Before you can indulge your sexual self, though, you need to become sexually aware. This means noticing what goes on in your body and developing erogenous awareness which allows you to recognise sensory experiences. Good feelings associated with touch are not all sexual, but they may lead to, or enhance, sexual feelings. Modern sex-therapy programmes focus on developing sensual awareness long before any sexual action takes place. Some sex therapists like to use mindfulness techniques which help the individual to focus on their senses in the here and now. Try the exercise below on developing mindful awareness to heighten your sensory recognition and improve your mindfulness skills. This is an outdoor exercise; an indoor mindfulness exercise is included on page 91.

EXERCISE: DEVELOPING MINDFUL AWARENESS

➤ In the garden, park or on a beach, sit on a chair or bench and remove your shoes and socks.

➤ Become aware of your breathing. Is it rapid or unhurried? Shallow or deep? Can you slow it down to a gentle rhythm?

➤ Place your feet on the ground and be aware of the feelings under your feet. If there is grass beneath them, does it feel scratchy or soft? Is it wet or dry and crackly? Do you like the feeling? If you feel a pathway rather than grass, is it hard and unyielding? If there is sand, can you bury your feet in it? Does it feel hot and painful or cool and soothing? Is it easy to keep your feet there or do you want to move them?

➤ Close your eyes and relax. Notice what you feel. You are already aware of the ground beneath your feet and the sensations of the grass or the pathway, but what else are you touching? Is the bench hard against your body or are you able to recline against a pillow or in a deckchair? Does this feel safe? Comfortable? Could you fall asleep?

➤ Notice how you are resting your hands and elbows. Are they relaxed or tense? What are they touching? Is your head supported? How tense is your neck? Scan your body and notice how you have arranged it and how this feels.

➤ Do you have any aches or pains? Does your tummy feel excited or anxious? Is it churning or quiet?

➤ How does the air feel around you? Is there a breeze? Is it hot or cold?

➤ What can you hear? Notice the sounds of wind, birds, traffic, your own breathing.

➤ Stay in the moment, noticing everything around you ...

Mindfulness exercises enhance sexual awareness as they may help you to be more conscious of touch and arousal. The more aware you become of yourself and the more comfortable you are with your own views and feelings, the more able you are to see other people's point of views, including your partner's. By developing comfort with yourself and your sexual expression, you have more time to devote to your relationship, rather than being distracted by your personal insecurities and concerns. As we shall see in the next part of the book, keeping your relationship alive doesn't happen automatically. The assumptions, experience and emotional baggage you bring to the relationship are bound to affect it, so the more you recognise and deal with your own concerns, the more space you will have to develop your sexual and emotional connection and to recognise and overcome any problems developing between you.

Part Two
Sexual Coupledom

Chapter Four
Keeping Your Relationship Alive

Once you are in a committed relationship, naturally you hope your connection will deepen and grow. You probably assume that if problems do develop, the strength of your relationship will be able to deal with whatever comes along. However, you may quickly develop unhelpful habits within the relationship which are difficult to change. Often these are related to ways of communicating which become embedded before you know it. A common approach, for instance, is to try to avoid talking about issues which bother you, hoping they will iron themselves out or that a better time to discuss them will somehow emerge. The longer this continues, the harder it is to lose the habit or address the troubling issue. It is even more difficult if some sort of sexual matter is involved, as you may be reluctant to hurt your partner's feelings or admit that you haven't been entirely honest.

CASE EXAMPLE: TRUDY AND GREG

Trudy had been in a few long-term and sexually satisfying relationships when she met Greg. They got along brilliantly and, after a few weeks, they began sleeping together. Trudy loved the closeness and sense of belonging this

---

brought and was really pleased their relationship had moved on. However, she was a little disappointed at how brief their sexual encounters were, with very little foreplay. They kissed and cuddled afterwards, which was lovely, but Trudy did not have an orgasm or even feel very aroused.

Greg seemed unaware of this. However, he did tell Trudy he felt considerable anxiety about his sexual performance, though he said he had previously had good sexual relationships. Because of this, Trudy assumed Greg just needed some encouragement, so she pretended to be sexually aroused to orgasm. When nothing changed, Trudy tried to talk to Greg about ways of improving their experience, but he became so upset that she hadn't the heart to tell him she had been faking. She convinced herself that orgasms weren't important, but she felt as though she was cheating on Greg by pretending and she longed for a more intimate sexual experience. She could tell their lovemaking meant a lot to Greg, but she found it very mechanical.

Eventually, she blurted out the truth during an argument over, of all things, curtain material. In the aftermath, they both realised how badly they had needed to talk, especially as Trudy's secret spilled out so easily. Greg made an appointment for couple counselling, even though he expected the counsellor would side with Trudy and think he was a bad lover. On the contrary, the counsellor thought, perhaps, their relationship was so special to them both that they were afraid to take the risk of discussing what was bothering them.

In talking it through, the couple felt there was something in this. Greg was avoiding foreplay in case he got it wrong. He had hoped Trudy would tell him what she liked; as she appeared to love penetration, he had concentrated on this. Trudy, of course, had been trying not to hurt Greg so, without admitting what she was feeling the situation was never going to change. Realising this made a huge difference to the couple's confidence, allowing them to find ways to communicate through talk and touch and to make their lovemaking more intimate and satisfying for both of them.

'IN A RELATIONSHIP'

You probably wouldn't think of yourself as being dishonest in your relationship, but the case of Trudy and Greg illustrates how easy it is to find yourself in a situation where you aren't being frank but can't see an easy way to start being more open. This has become even more of an issue recently for many young couples. These days, sexual relationships often begin long before partners actually start calling themselves a couple. Some of this seems to be due to a desire to get the circumstances right before making any sort of commitment. Another reason is the lack of privacy couples experience now that many of us document everything we do on social media sites, such as Facebook. It is understandable to want to be as sure as possible before admitting to being 'in a relationship' if a break-up is likely to be played out publicly. This can be particularly true for couples in second long-term relationships whose children, friends and family may be observing their online profiles with interest.

However, emotions can't just be switched on and off, and you may be one of many couples who were actually incredibly close by the time they decided to go public. Yet, throughout the time you have been together you may have felt it was awkward or inappropriate to discuss any problems, especially sexual ones, if the relationship wasn't official or going anywhere. Indeed, you may have felt it would drive your partner away. Once the relationship seems more committed, though, it may be hard to know how to start airing stale issues and making complaints without disclosing that you have been pretending all along. Consequently, by the time you do get round to admitting you are an item, bad habits are already long established.

Ironically, intimacy is often a casualty when relationships become officially closer. While it is thought of as not really a relationship, or while it remains private, there is so much less strain to conform to ideas that may not suit you at all. Once the relationship is in the spotlight, however, there is even more demand to get it right. All of a sudden, there are rules and, maybe, awareness of difficulties which weren't there before. Where intimacy may have blossomed, it is now constrained by all the conventions that come with being in a serious relationship. Unhelpful beliefs may pop up too. For instance, you may believe that you wouldn't have sexual problems if the relationship were good enough. Some people seem to believe that relationships have magical qualities. If you believe that being in a relationship should be enough to make everything okay, it is a shock to discover that it isn't.

Adapting

Even if you have seen yourselves as a couple right from the start, you may be reluctant to rock the boat at the beginning. This can lead to ignoring your own needs or wishes, hoping the time will come when they sort themselves out. For instance, faking orgasm doesn't always work out as well as it did for Trudy and Greg. Sometimes it feels impossible to admit faking, and the longer it continues the more difficult it is to acknowledge what has been happening. This is discussed in more detail on page 176.

However, most couples develop some difficulties with sexuality or intimacy at some point, even when they manage to be frank from the outset. In particular, it is a real challenge for every couple to construct a way of being together intimately while still being able to grow and develop as individuals.

Even if things are great between the two of you at the start, both of you need to be able to adapt to the differences life throws at you and not feel threatened by the other's needs, or, indeed, your own. The longer you know one another, the more life is likely to intrude. For instance, it is fine to stay up all night making love when you have few responsibilities and can have a weekend lie-in, but something else when you have jobs, a household to manage and children who wake at 5am.

Being aware that life can encroach on the relationship can make problems seem less of a challenge when they occur. Accepting that you may need to seek solutions, both together and separately, places you halfway to dealing with the situation since worry about having a problem is often much more distressing than the problem itself.

Expecting too much

Unfortunately, many of us are unprepared for relationship problems and think our issues should solve themselves. You may expect each other to provide all the emotional support and comfort you need in your life – to be best friends, share all the same interests and spend your leisure time together. However, both individuals and their relationships are dynamic, developing different styles and needs as experience affects them, so it doesn't work to try to be the same. Indeed, this is both a recipe for boredom and a passion killer; you may end up feeling more like brother and sister than lovers. Some young and inexperienced couples also expect sex to naturally lead to simultaneous orgasm, following about half an hour of intercourse. They are unaware that, unlike in the movies, very few couples experience orgasm at the same time and that intercourse usually only involves a few minutes of continuous thrusting.

Whether your sex life has never met your expectations or has lost its sparkle more recently, being unafraid to look at your own thoughts and feelings is a very positive first step towards addressing this and how to go about making any changes you feel are needed. You may have avoided doing so because it can be hard to know how to get started or you may even worry that your concerns aren't reasonable. Change is always possible, but you may need help – at the very least, you need to be talking to one another.

LIVING TOGETHER

Missing your old life can be a genuine problem if you are a couple who feels you have to do everything together once you have moved in with each other. It can be puzzling and disappointing to discover that life together isn't as blissful as expected. Most people have family, friends or activities which they need to engage with in order to top up their sense of wellbeing, but you may neglect these or find them difficult to fit in. Couples in long-distance relationships may have spent years pining for the same address, only to find it frustratingly difficult to adapt to being with their partner day in, day out. Often the relationship is blamed, rather than the circumstances. You begin to notice habits and dwell on small issues which were previously easy to overlook. Rather than admit that you need to allow yourselves more space, and find a way to achieve that, you blame one another and become very unhappy.

It is often this prevailing feeling that we *ought* to love one another's company, and have no difficulty being in each other's pockets, which makes it so difficult to do. If you believe this is the way it ought to be, it is hard to admit that it isn't like that. You may be afraid of hurting your partner's feelings or worried that there is something wrong with you. So any conversations you have to try to solve things end up being about the relationship not working rather than about how you can cope with the very demanding process of learning to live together. Focusing your conversations on achieving the positive outcome you are seeking, rather than blaming yourself or your partner for what has gone on, is a purposeful and constructive way to go. After all, the past has gone and can't be changed, but you *can* use your past experience to help you plan for the future and recognise potential snags and pitfalls.

Managing differences

While some couples want to be together constantly, others fear the relationship will take them over. Observation of other relationships may convince you that your needs or personality will disappear. You may be particularly concerned if you notice that those around you seem to have unequal partnerships, where one appears to be getting more from the relationship than the other.

The most successful relationships make space for each partner to develop in their own way. As the last chapter explained, feeling permitted to explore your own thoughts and feelings, and feeling able to continue to enjoy different activities from your partner allow you to feel more confident. You are less likely to be bored with one another if you each bring fresh ideas and experiences to the relationship. Your own sense of personal growth makes it possible for the relationship to flourish alongside. The feeling that you always have someone on your side, and not working against you, allows the security of the relationship to become really embedded. If, on the other hand, you are struggling to think the same and be the same, you are bound to run into difficulties eventually because no two people are exactly alike. As we shall see in the next chapter, we all bring different experiences, beliefs and needs to our relationships, and we have to accommodate these without feeling threatened or undermined.

CASE EXAMPLE: KAREN AND CALUM

Dark-haired Karen had always wanted a short blonde hairstyle and was thrilled when her friends told her how great she looked when she had her hair cut and dyed lighter. Her partner, Calum, was not immediately enthusiastic, however, telling her he would need some time to get used to the look. Karen was angry with Calum and very hurt. She called the hairdresser immediately to see how soon she would be able to change the colour.

Karen felt that she needed Calum to affirm her choices. Instead of recognising that her friends liked her hairstyle and that *she* liked her hairstyle, she allowed herself to be both furious and hurt. Perhaps Calum was insensitive. Or perhaps he was the sort of person who needed time to adapt to any change. Karen wasn't thinking about this. She could only think about how Calum had let her down and, simultaneously, how she had got it so wrong.

She could have waited to see if her new colour *did* grow on Calum before changing it. Some people would have just assumed that Calum would like it eventually. If Karen had more confidence in herself and her choices, she would not have cared so much about Calum's response because *she* would have been satisfied that her hair looked great. She might also have been able to think about the reasons why Calum responded the way he did and tried to understand them. Then she may not have felt so personally assaulted.

CASE EXAMPLE: JIM AND ANDY

When Jim took Andy to a concert, he was pleased that Andy seemed to be enjoying himself, as this was Jim's favourite kind of music. Afterwards, Andy said he had found the evening quite pleasant and thanked Jim for taking him, but commented that this style of music wasn't really his cup of tea.

Jim felt rejected, was livid and started to walk off, saying there was no point in continuing the relationship. Andy was apologetic but baffled; he didn't understand why his opinion was *so* important to Jim.

Some people are not unduly bothered if their partner doesn't agree with them; others, like Karen and Jim in the case examples, feel truly devastated if their partner does not like what they like and does not affirm their views and choices. If matters like hairstyles and music can come between couples, the potential for conflict over sexual difficulties is enormous. The way round this is not to get quite so het up over differences of opinion unless they really are important. In other words, don't just react; choose your battles with great care.

Sharing interests and spending so much time together is relatively new. In the past, couples used to spend much more time apart pursuing their own interests. They didn't automatically expect to spend that much leisure time together, if they even had any. People didn't usually move as far from their childhood home either, so relatives and friends tended to be closer by and more available when partners were busy.

Accepting that you don't need to be joined at the hip and that differences are inevitable may be difficult if being together constantly is what everyone seems to expect. However, this one-size-fits-all approach to relationships doesn't take into account the individual wants and needs of you and your partner. Furthermore, it does nothing to encourage communication, which can easily lead to misunderstandings. Trying to understand each other's viewpoint, even if you don't agree, makes flare-ups in the relationship less likely and encourages the development of intimacy. Let's face it, you aren't going to feel much like sex or a cuddle if you are constantly at war over trivia. Try the quiz below to see how good you are at managing difference in your relationship.

QUIZ: HOW DO YOU MANAGE DIFFERENCE?

1. You are out with friends and your partner disagrees with your view of the film you have just seen. Do you:
   a) Join a lively debate about the merits of the movie?
   b) Appeal to your friends to agree with you?
   c) Feel upset and sulk?
   d) Shrug – who cares what anyone else thinks anyway?

2. You are in bed together and feeling very aroused when your partner develops pins and needles in their leg. Do you:
   a) Massage the affected leg until the tingling wears off and take up where you left off?
   b) Go and make a cup of tea?
   c) Tell your partner they spoil everything and say you're going to sleep?
   d) Laugh?

3. Your partner comes home from work and, unusually, says they want to go out for a walk or run before talking to you. Do you:

a) Wonder if there is something wrong and start making dinner while you wait for them to come back?

b) Say you'll come too and follow them out?

c) Let them go, but feel resentful because you've had a long day too, and then don't talk when they get back?

d) Go out for the evening with your friends?

4. Your partner says they are thinking of going away without you on a weekend sports trip with their team. Do you:

a) Hope they have a good time and start planning what you'll do when they are away?

b) Insist you will come along too to cheer them along, even though you hate the sport?

c) Tell them it isn't fair to leave you alone and they can't go?

d) Book a longer trip away with an old flame?

5. Your partner's mother breaks an ornament while visiting. She is clearly embarrassed and offers to pay for it. Do you:

a) Thank her and accept the money?

b) Insist you can't accept the money but privately feel resentful?

c) Complain to your partner about how clumsy she is?

d) Take the money but say you never liked that ornament anyway?

6. You have gone away for the weekend and assume you
   will be making love. After dinner on the Friday night,
   you make it clear you are interested in sex but your
   partner says they are too tired. Do you:
   a) Have a cuddle instead and hope they will be less
      tired in the morning?
   b) Say it doesn't matter, but cry yourself to sleep?
   c) Explain how hurtful this is and refuse to make
      love for the rest of the weekend?
   d) Go to the bathroom and masturbate?

Mostly As
You are able to deal with disappointment even when it
makes you unhappy. One reason is that you don't need
your partner to validate your views and behaviour and you
don't assume your partner is being deliberately hurtful
when the two of you disagree.

Mostly Bs
You probably feel that you put up with a lot. You often feel
judged so even when you feel really bad you don't like
to share how you're feeling. Sometimes, though, your
upset gets blurted out during a row. Rather than being
direct, you try to find other ways, such as dropping hints
or coercion, to get what you want or need – not always
successfully.

Mostly Cs
You often react before you think. You are easily offended and
take it to heart when others disagree with you. You believe

that rowing clears the air, but you also think that your partner should know how you feel. Consequently, you are often upset when your partner can't guess what you want.

Mostly Ds
You generally don't like to show your feelings. You wouldn't dream of telling your partner what you need or asking for anything. This means that you appear to take care of yourself and not to be bothered when your partner doesn't agree with you. Consequently, your behaviour can sometimes come across as a little thoughtless.

One of the problems you will have if you find it hard to deal with disappointment and difference is that you either tend to focus on your feelings too much or ignore them altogether. An alternative way of thinking is to try to look more objectively at the evidence for what is going on. This may help you to believe that what is happening is not meant as a personal insult to you.

People rarely intend to be mean, but it is very easy to misunderstand one another and assume that hurt is intentional, particularly if you are not completely honest. If you are relying on your partner to make you feel okay, rather than learning how to look after yourself, you will always be at a disadvantage. This is not to say that couples should be inconsiderate, but nor should they rely on each other to mind-read or walk on eggshells.

How problems develop
As we saw in Part One, differences of opinion over when to make love can be a major stressor in relationships. Managing this is even more difficult if you haven't found a way to communicate generally about

your differences or if you misunderstand one another. Recognising when the other partner is interested in sex can be a challenge which often emerges after couples move in together. It isn't always easy to find time to fit in lovemaking or to be clear if that is what your partner wants. Sexual cues are lost over time or are never properly established. Hence, the way communication develops early on can affect how able you will be to communicate effectively in future (see more about communication in Chapter Fourteen, pages 201–220). This is when the seeds of sexual problems are sown and when performance anxiety can first begin to get in the way.

Losing an erection, failure to orgasm or coming too soon are often one-off events which can be put down to tiredness or too much alcohol and be easily forgotten. However, worrying about them or taking them personally can begin a more serious and enduring problem if you are unable to support one another.

Rather than being able to provide their own feelings of self-worth, lack of confidence about their own wishes can make some people feel low unless their partner convincingly reassures them. Small problems are more likely to become big issues if you are expecting your partner to make you feel okay. The trouble is that constantly asking for reassurance can be irritating, but, if you don't ask, your partner may not know when it is needed. Moreover, if you require your partner to make you feel good about your sexual self, and to be responsible for your sexual wellbeing and orgasm, you are effectively giving away your sexual control. This doesn't mean that you should cease to give one another sexual pleasure. On the contrary, it means you should develop ways of helping one another to do so effectively, but without blaming or minding too much if it doesn't all go perfectly to plan. Couples who feel they manage their relationship successfully are able to support one another when it is necessary without their own self-esteem being affected. This means being able to support yourself first but able to seek and give help when it is needed. This often seems easier at the beginning of relationships when your focus may be more on enjoying your new partner than worries about yourself.

THE HONEYMOON PERIOD

Nostalgia for the honeymoon period of their relationship is what often brings couples to therapy. They come with the aim of recapturing the feelings and sexual behaviour they once enjoyed. However, quite a bit will have changed.

At the beginning, when you don't know one another anything like so well, you are on the alert for signs that your partner is the ideal person, the one you have always been looking for. It is easy to find such signs when you only see someone in short bursts and you are probably both on your best behaviour anyway. On dates you are both totally focused on one another, with few distractions. Once you move in together, and even more so when you start a family, there are any number of other demands upon your time and energy.

When you were dating, there may have been an expectation that cuddles and/or sex would be part of every meeting. You probably made a point of making time for this. When you are living together, you can make love whenever you want to – so the same pressure isn't there to do it. Consequently, nurturing the relationship and finding time for lovemaking may slip way down the list of your priorities.

The 'cuddle hormone'

Early-days' sex is part of the bonding process, when nature is doing its best to make you pair up. Added to this is the influence of the hormone oxytocin, which is present in the body in high levels during the early part of relationships. It has been called the 'cuddle hormone' because it promotes trust, closeness and bonding. It is thought to occur at such high levels when relationships are new to encourage pairing and mating. It is also thought to reduce fear and anxiety, so it may lessen any doubts you have about the relationship.

In association with the hormone vasopressin, oxytocin is additionally thought to make you pay more attention to the aspects of your partner that you are attracted to and not to notice problems. It increases your self-confidence – one of the reasons we feel so good about ourselves when relationships are new. Serotonin is another chemical which is found in the body in high levels during the early part of relationships and is responsible for making you feel more socially confident, more relaxed but also more obsessed with your new partner. Pheromones are chemicals released by the body which make you more attractive; these are also high in the early stages of relationships and when you are sexually active.

WHEN EARLY EUPHORIA WEARS OFF

You can't maintain these hormones and feelings for all that long. For most people, the early euphoria has worn off within a year or two at most. So, though you can't get the early-days' hormones back in the same way later in the relationship, a network of chemicals continues to work to keep you together as a couple. Indeed, you can encourage the release of oxytocin into the body by allowing yourself to feel aroused and anticipating sex.

Arousal releases oxytocin, which, in association with the hormone vasopressin, promotes feelings of calm and satisfaction by reducing levels of cortisol, which is associated with stress. This means that the more you allow yourself to feel aroused, and to remember and look forward to lovemaking, the more oxytocin you will release. So partners who look for frequent sex have a point. The longer you go without making love, the less likely it is that you will want to. Having said that, periods of separation and abstinence increase desire if you keep thinking positively about your partner, anticipate lovemaking and allow yourself to feel aroused.

To make up for the lower levels of oxytocin as your relationship progresses, the hormone vasopressin, which is released alongside oxytocin, is thought to help increase bonding. It appears that the more it is released when couples are together, the more they like each other. Significantly, it may be released during any joint activity with your partner. As we have seen, this definitely includes sex, but could also involve everyday activities such as childcare and housework! The pleasure hormone dopamine continues to be released when you have sex, laugh or do anything which you enjoy. It also 'remembers' the activity, encouraging you to do it more – another reason for keeping your sex life active.

If early sex was for bonding, there are inevitably other reasons why we continue to feel desire as relationships progress. There are numerous reasons for wanting sex and only some of them are concerned with sexual pleasure, romance, love or reproduction. The list below states reasons for having sex. Consider which of them apply to you. We don't tend to talk openly about the assortment of incentives for sex – but there are probably as many motives as there are people. It can be surprising to realise that there is such a range of reasons for engaging in sex, usually with more than one providing motivation. For instance, you may mistrust what you think your partner's reasons are but you'll probably be surprised to discover that your own reasons are quite wide-ranging and, sometimes, unromantic. See how many more you can add to the list.

- To deepen the relationship
- To express love
- To have fun
- To please your partner
- To please yourself
- To shut your partner up
- To stop your partner having sex with someone else

- To feel close
- To feel loved
- To feel attractive
- To feel wanted
- To feel more masculine/feminine
- To feel in control
- Because it is a duty
- Because you feel entitled to
- To increase your bargaining power
- To increase your power
- To say sorry
- To make a baby
- To manage stress
- To have an orgasm

At the beginning of your relationship, you probably made love because you wanted to feel close and bonded and because you were attracted to your partner. Some of the other reasons may have existed too – such as feeling wanted or attractive – but the list grows as the relationship continues. This may come as a surprise if you thought that love and baby-making were the main or only reasons for wanting to make love.

Some people do worry that they want to make love for the wrong reasons and are fearful about what this could mean for their relationship. Some individuals and couples with perfectly happy, well-functioning relationships come to counselling just because they are questioning their motivation and worrying that their thinking has some negative significance. Similarly, making love less than you feel you ought to may make you feel there is something wrong with you, your partner or the relationship. If you are on the lookout for problems, it is very easy to misread your partner's behaviour or meaning and feel rejected. For instance, when your partner says they are too tired for sex, they probably really do mean just that.

Making time

Many people look forward to lovemaking as an affirmation of their worth and a way of helping them to relax. This doesn't work so well if your partner can't wind down as well. For instance, if they are thinking about work, getting the children up for swimming lessons early in the morning, doing the shopping and having in-laws over for Sunday lunch, de-stressing you with sex may not be a top priority. An early night may be.

When you were first together you may have enjoyed weekend mornings in bed with the newspapers, drinking coffee and making love before a leisurely stroll to the pub and an unhurried Sunday lunch. However, as your circumstances change, managing to squeeze in the time for lovemaking may become more difficult. Weekends may be the only time for housework, children's activities, shopping or catching up with friends and family, and the diary can become very full very quickly. As you progress in your career, weekend mornings may be needed for catching up with work or preparing for the new week. Older parents may need a visit or come to you at weekends. You yourselves may have new hobbies that require weekend attention. You may each work clashing shifts or organise work patterns so that one of you is always available for childcare. Or you may just be too exhausted to do anything much on your days off. Finding the time for lovemaking is a constant challenge which couples need to address realistically. It may be something that you have to sit down and plan, or you may need to experiment with different times to find out what works.

Spontaneity

Countless couples seen at Relate say they want to return spontaneity to their sex life. However, sex is never *really* spontaneous. There is so much to take into consideration, quite apart from finding the time and having the privacy to relax together. For a start, you want to be clean if you are going to be physically close with someone. Apart from finding a grubby partner a turn-off, *you* probably won't feel so sensual and relaxed if you are sweaty or worried about being smelly. For instance, though you may be keen on the idea of making love first thing in the morning, it is likely to be even better if you brush your teeth first.

Managing menstruation may be another area where a kind of sexual etiquette needs to be developed as to what is and is not acceptable. Some women feel more like sex when they are menstruating but they and/or their partner don't like the mess or the smell associated with menstruation. Though manual (pleasuring with the hands), anal and oral sex are still possible when you are menstruating, some women feel under the weather around the time of their period. There may also be cultural or religious practices to observe. This is something you both need to be clear about and respect each other's feelings. Unless culturally prohibited, you can still make this time great for snuggles if not for sex, which then becomes even more special to look forward to.

Contraception can be a similar bar to spontaneity; this is a reason why some people don't like to use condoms. However, putting on a condom can become an enjoyable part of the lovemaking process. Reaching for a condom can also be used as a signal that a woman is becoming aroused enough for penetration – or has just had her first orgasm.

Boredom

Having to plan and make time for sex can actually make the encounters more reliably enjoyable. Indeed, those carefree early memories may not be all that dependable. Though you may have delighted in each other's bodies and company, sometimes excitement, novelty and hormones prevent any attention to negatives. Now you have more comfort and space to genuinely explore together.

The idea of exploration and discovery doesn't seem to feature in some long-term relationships, however. There is an expectation for many people that boredom will set in after a few years. Yet there is no reason for this to be inevitable. So-called 'boredom' really occurs because couples make assumptions about one another and stop being curious and interested. Letting time pass without stating your wants or needs, trying to be too similar and assuming that anything new won't be of interest to your partner are probably among the main reasons for sexual stagnation.

If you have developed an intimate relationship and feel comfortable talking to one another, concerns can be addressed as they occur rather than being ignored. Intimate couples are likely to feel enabled to grow and develop personally too, so they are not so similar that there is nothing much of interest to discuss or discover. Indeed, there may be considerably more to learn than you imagined, as the next chapter explains.

Chapter Five
The Sexual Dowry

Few couples stop to seriously consider the way sexual patterns have developed in their relationship. Most of us just assume that whatever has happened was inevitable and it doesn't occur to us that there are reasons for the way we behave. For instance, you may not be aware of the differences in the attitudes and upbringing between yourself and your partner if these seem alike on the surface. It is much easier to notice some of the cultural differences between partners who were brought up in different countries and who have different religions and customs. The cultural differences between partners who were raised in apparently similar circumstances are much more difficult to recognise, making them powerful undercover troublemakers.

The messages and conventions we absorb as we grow up seem as natural to us as breathing. They affect the way we think and behave, our attitudes and beliefs, and this influences the way we perceive other people's intentions and meanings. Because sex can be treated as a delicate – and even secretive – subject in many families, it is an area where misinterpretation and misunderstandings in relationships is particularly likely.

COMFORT WITH AFFECTION

Families' level of comfort with intimacy and affection varies significantly too. Some families are extremely tactile, thinking nothing of hugging, kissing and sprinkling one another with 'I love yous.' If you are from a family like this, you may find it hard to understand why your partner is more reserved and becomes uncomfortable, or even embarrassed, by physical displays of affection. Each of you is likely to assume that your way is the right way, which can lead to irritability and hurt feelings.

It is understandable that couples reproduce the relationship examples offered by their own parents – that is what they know. You may realise that, even when you decide to do things differently, you often find yourself behaving like your mum or dad. Despite trying not to, there are probably some family behaviours and character traits that you aren't aware of.

We all acquire 'scripts' about how to behave in different situations. Though we may be unaware of them, these scripts inevitably affect our expectations and understanding. Usually, the script is so normal to us that we assume everyone else sees things the same way too. Of course, they don't. The case example of Will and Ewan demonstrates how easy it is to get the wrong end of the stick.

CASE EXAMPLE: WILL AND EWAN

The couple met on a business training scheme for graduates and hit it off straight away. They were both keen divers and were delighted to find they had been on diving holidays in similar places and had a similar level of skill. Both their fathers were accountants and they were both brought up in the suburbs of cities in the north of England – Will in Manchester and Ewan in Leeds.

Initially, Ewan loved the way Will could talk to anyone comfortably and animatedly. He was delighted that Will always had his arm round him and would hug, grab, squeeze and kiss him whenever he was feeling enthusiastic or excited about anything, as well as when he wanted to show affection. After a while, though, Ewan started to find the constant touching intrusive. Will was slightly more restrained at work but very touchy-feely if they were out together and Ewan started to complain that Will was constantly pawing him.

Will, meanwhile, accused Ewan of being buttoned up and aggressive because he never kissed or touched Will spontaneously at home, unless they were in a sexual situation. He would tolerate a kiss if they were meeting or leaving each other but never initiated touching otherwise.

Matters came to a head when Will's sister came to visit and Ewan pushed her away when she hugged him. Will accused him of rudeness and Ewan said Will's family was weird. From then on, they were both on the lookout for examples of rudeness and weirdness so their relationship became a constant battleground. It wasn't until Will's mother casually pointed out the difference in the families' comfort with intimacy that they began to understand what was happening.

When they really thought about it, they became aware that, although Ewan's family were extremely welcoming and smiley, they were more likely to shake hands on meeting than to hug. They also realised that, though Will's family were mostly big huggers, Will's father was less demonstrative than the others. Will had never really noticed before that it was his mother's side of the family who were most physically expressive and decided to talk to his parents about this.

Will's parents proved to be very helpful in explaining how his father had adapted to the difference in their ways of showing affection. His father had loved the slightly chaotic and free way they expressed themselves, but nevertheless sometimes found it a bit overwhelming and difficult to join in with. He pointed out how awkward it must be for Ewan and Ewan was able to see that Will was not setting out to annoy or embarrass him. They realised that neither of them had thought the way they behaved was unusual, so they just hadn't bothered to consider the effect they were each having on the other.

Will and Ewan's example shows how easily we can slip into habitual ways of thinking which don't take into account our partner's point of view. Rather than accepting your first thoughts about a situation, it is always helpful to challenge your own assumptions and wonder about some alternatives. It doesn't matter if you don't hit on the 'correct' explanation straight away – even realising that other reasons for a situation *could* possibly exist can stop you from feeling hurt or becoming angry. It is much more helpful to explain your position calmly than to allow yourself to bottle up your feelings and become more and more resentful. Assuming that you both think the same way is what leads to the sort of difficulty Will and Ewan experienced.

Sometimes beliefs are so common around us that they become accepted as facts and affect the way we behave. Because the ideas are so established we aren't aware enough to question them, so they persist. Behaviours can also become established stealthily. Couples tend to just slip into a routine that isn't talked about and they develop expectations about who does what. For instance, at night Michael locks the doors and Pamela makes a bedtime drink. This becomes a habit which satisfies them both. However, sometimes couples continue with roles they hate, probably becoming grumpy as a result.

SHAME ABOUT FEELINGS

Not only do everyday feelings and exchanges affect couples' desire to be sexual together, but a similar dynamic can exist around sex itself. We absorb subtle messages about sex and the way we treat our bodies. These may have been prevalent in our culture or religion and consequently shared by most of the people we grew up with.

The attitude of your family to your body and sex will inevitably influence your feelings about them. Some families are very open and tolerant while others are embarrassed and restricted in their attitudes. Individuals respond differently to their family's behaviour too. For instance, some people feel permanently affected by an embarrassing incident in their past, such as being caught masturbating, even when they feel their families have been encouraging and enabling towards their sexual development.

Just as many of us don't notice our family's influence on the way we think and feel, so we may not be aware that we are affected by culture. We often see culture as being about difference, affecting only people from abroad or whose parents were born elsewhere. This is because we don't notice the prevailing culture; it is the invisibility of the culture you grow up with that makes it so powerful.

The attitudes and beliefs of those around us, reinforced by the media, state or church, are continually affecting our own outlook and viewpoints. It is only to be expected that views which are everywhere are taken for granted, so we don't realise any influence exists. The attitudes and way of being we develop are so ordinary and natural to us that we are completely unaware there could be an alternative way of thinking.

Despite the effect of early experiences, this probably isn't something you are likely to think about very often. The exercise below may help to clarify where some of your ideas and beliefs about sex originated. Share what you discover with your partner to see how similar or different your experience has been. This may help you to understand differences in your thinking and how this affects your relationship.

EXERCISE: SEX EDUCATION

➤ How did you learn about sex? How much of this was from formal sex education, family, friends, your partner or books and the media? Which of these was most/least helpful?

➤ Did you feel prepared for puberty?

➤ How do you think the changes in your body as you grew up affected you?

➤ What was your family's reaction to these changes?

➤ Who in your family is most/least comfortable discussing sex?

➤ Has the way you manage your family's attitude to sex changed since you have been grown up?

➤ If you have children, in what ways do you feel you are recreating your family's attitudes?

➤ Growing up, who did you turn to if you had a concern about your body or sexuality?

➤ Who would you turn to now?

➤ To what extent does your family's approval of your sexuality matter to you?

➤ How much do you think your attitudes are influenced by your religion or culture?

Many couples are surprised by their own answers to some of these questions and realise that they have never really understood or considered their own motivation and experience. It can also be a revelation to discover that your surface similarities conceal differences in your outlook and backgrounds, which may account for some of the misunderstandings in your relationship. It is fascinating to notice whether, or how, boys and girls were treated differently in your families, as this alone can influence your expectations and understanding in your adult sexual relationships.

GENDER ISSUES

Many partners – particularly women – don't feel they ought to have sexual needs, but believe they should be responsible for their partner's sexual pleasure. As a result they feel guilty if they are not feeling sexually available. The more they don't say what they are thinking or state their needs, the more sex becomes an activity for the partner rather than for them and the more resentment is liable to grow on both sides.

Similarly, some people feel a little ashamed of their sexual feelings. Whereas men are more likely to feel ashamed about lack of sexual feelings, women often worry that they may be seen as 'easy' or sexually voracious. Such feelings may prevent you from developing your own sexual style, embracing the needs and wishes you could discover if you would only allow yourself to do so.

Instead, in some straight relationships there is a tacit understanding that the man is the one with an unquenchable sexual thirst. Equally, a man may avoid initiating sexual situations out of a belief that his needs are too much for his partner, who then feels obliged to agree. Or you may be a man who finds it difficult to make love to a woman you respect, especially if sex feels a little dirty. It may be even harder once she becomes a mother. Each of these possibilities is very common, but difficult for partners to effectively address.

Try the exercise below on how expectations affect sexual expression to see how your attitudes about your gender could be affecting you. The way you treat yourself and your partner with regard to gender is sure to be influenced by what you expect from each other's gender roles. Remember, these attitudes are potentially hidden – from yourself as well as your partner – as we don't normally think about them. We do, however, live them.

EXERCISE: HOW EXPECTATIONS AFFECT SEXUAL EXPRESSION

➤ What are the roles you feel you should be fulfilling in order to be a 'proper' man/woman?

➤ What roles do you feel your partner should be fulfilling in order to be a 'proper' man/woman?

➤ How do these roles differ from what you actually want to be doing?

➤ What is the sexual behaviour you feel is appropriate for your gender?

➤ What is the sexual behaviour you feel is appropriate for your partner's gender?

➤ How do these roles differ from what you actually want to be doing?

➤ How would you feel if you changed your behaviour to be more in keeping with what you want to do rather than what you ought to do?

➤ How would your partner feel if you changed your behaviour to be more in keeping with what you want to do rather than what you ought to do?

➤ Is there anything you feel your partner might like to do differently?

➤ What do you think is stopping you both from changing?

Talking about the exercise questions with your partner, or even with friends and family, may help to clarify your thinking and help you to be more the way you want to be rather than the way you think you should be. Worrying about getting it wrong can actually hinder rather than help your sex life. While consideration for your partner is important, being scared to identify or admit your own needs, or to take small risks, can result in sexual boredom. You may be frightened that mentioning any changes will upset your partner. This is a great reason to get into the habit of discussing what is and isn't working for you early in the relationship. When matters are left unaddressed you may reach a stage where you don't even know what you want or need any more. When this happens you may also reach a position where you are unable to challenge sexual and gender scripts because you are so unaware of them.

If the previous exercise has made you wonder if it would be possible to change, perhaps you would enjoy the 'sexual sentry' talking point below. Use this to begin a conversation with your partner about the way your upbringing and scripts are affecting your potential to enjoy being sexual together. You may also want to consider how you answered the questions about sex in the previous exercise. Ask yourself why you answered the way you did. What evidence is there for your point of view?

TALKING POINT: THE SEXUAL SENTRY

➤ What ideas or beliefs put the brakes on your sexual expression?

➤ How does that happen?

➤ What is allowed?

➤ Who has influenced your beliefs about your sexuality and sexual expression in the past?

➤ Who influences your beliefs about your sexuality and sexual expression now?

These questions are very simple but not necessarily easy to answer as these aren't areas we normally consider. However, learning the habit of questioning your thinking and behaviour means you are much more ready to respond, and aware of what might be influencing you, when problems occur. Once you understand what is influencing your behaviour and thinking, you have the opportunity to accept or reject that way of being. It is unlikely that you and your partner are always going to be 100 per cent in agreement, but some couples feel they ought to be. Understanding where your differences lie, and why you have them, may help you to accept a little uncertainty and allow both of you to feel more confident that having your own point of view is no threat to the relationship. In fact, being really clear about who thinks what allows you both to take responsibility and not to blame each other for what you *imagine* the other wants or thinks.

PLEASING YOURSELF

It may come as a shock to realise that it is your own sexual script which is affecting your behaviour and that your partner doesn't necessarily share your expectations. When your sexual motivation is dictated by beliefs about one another's judgement, you are unlikely to have a truly fulfilling sex life. If you feel obliged to accommodate or avoid what you believe to be your partner's wishes, you won't have any energy left to recognise your own. As we shall see in the next chapter, worrying too much about pleasing your partner, or about your sexual performance, is what ultimately leads to many people's long-term sexual problems. At the root of this may not be a longing to make your partner happy, but instead a need for your partner's approval. Ironically, those who really yearn for connection with their partners are often among the worst at discussing their feelings and telling their partner what *they* need. Too often, communication is conducted in each individual's head rather than an actual discussion taking place, so that all reactions about the relationship, from joy to resentment, are actually based on guesswork.

It is common to be afraid to tell one another what you want or need in case the other person doesn't want it too. You may not value your own needs enough to feel confident about stating them, so you may behave as though you have no needs or wait for your partner to guess what they are. You may have to make a conscious effort to tell your partner what you want or feel. We can't read each other's minds and relying on guesswork is likely to make a tricky situation worse.

Some of us have grown up in families where needs are rarely stated or entertained. This is a common way of being in northern Europe and accounts for the British 'stiff upper lip' attitude. Resilience is certainly to be admired; however, it isn't brave or sensible to put up with anything that is harming you at worst or making you uncomfortable at best. Somehow, many of us have developed the idea that to show need is to invite rejection. Some people deal with this by trying to ensure they and their partner think and behave as one. You may refer to your partner as your soulmate and, on some level, be constantly on the lookout for evidence of your shared world view. Your barely conscious feeling is that your needs are the same, so they are nothing to be ashamed of. However, sexual needs are never exactly the same; no two minds or bodies are identical. Thinking this way dismisses a big part of what is special and fun about sex – connecting with another human being. You can't connect if you are enmeshed or if making the connection emphasises the separateness that so upsets you.

If this sounds like you, perhaps you could try the experiment of asking your partner for something and see how that goes. If asking for sexual favours or telling your partner what feels good makes you feel awkward, begin with a non-sexual request – a lift, a cup of tea, help with a chore. Notice how difficult this is to do and how comfortable – or uncomfortable – you feel with the response.

Think about whether it is just your partner you feel awkward with or whether it is everyone. If so, you could try explaining this to your partner too. They may then find it easier to help you out when you are struggling to say what you want. You may be surprised to find they need a hand to express themselves too.

Honesty and vulnerability

Sometimes, people who claim to have no needs come across as rather selfish, expecting their needs to be met rather than being able to either make requests for themselves or show appreciation of others. Instead, you may dismiss other people's attempts to please you or suggest you expected more. You may seem difficult to satisfy, but perhaps you feel others haven't made the effort you deserve. Rather than show your needs, you may genuinely believe you don't have any and may be intolerant of others' needs as well, particularly your partner's.

So that any lurking needs don't become too obvious, you may avoid sex. If you have hooked up with someone who wants to be closer, you may become caught in a push-me-pull-you dance as you both try to find the level of closeness that feels comfortable. Stories of high/low desire often surface to mask this (see page 22).

Intimacy requires us to be honest and vulnerable, which is not possible if you are trying to hide or dismiss your needs. It is only possible to be intimate if you are clearly two separate people meeting together. However, many couples spend a great deal of time, energy and distress striving to be the same person (soulmates) or running away. If this sounds like you, use the exercises earlier in the chapter to help you examine your motivation and needs. Your partner won't be able to understand you unless *you* can make some sense of yourself. Working out what you are trying to avoid is an excellent start. Fear of getting something wrong, of being overwhelmed by the relationship or of being hurt are all common reasons for avoiding intimacy. Finding a level of intimacy which feels comfortable and safe isn't possible if you aren't sure of your own needs, let alone your partner's. However, as soon as one of you behaves differently, the other will respond to this and the process of change will begin. Getting started is the hard part; sometimes the changes we know are necessary don't fit with the way we would like to see ourselves.

Nurturing self-image

Chapter Three looked at how your sexual image affects your ability to be sexual (see pages 31–44). Research has shown that the way you think about yourself affects your desire and arousal. Most people like to feel that others see them the way they would like to see themselves. This explains why we do, say and acquire things which enhance the image we are seeking. Of course, the sort of partner we have also affects our self-image and may be why partners often nag each other to change aspects of themselves.

If you feel that you and your partner are the same, or if you spend your time chasing or running away from intimacy with your partner, it is no surprise to find that positive feelings about yourself often plummet. Your self-image won't be so affected if you feel entitled to have needs while feeling unfazed by, and sensitive to, your partner's desires and wishes. If you have to be the same, neither of you can have your own needs – which is, in the end, impossible. You are effectively attempting to stop existing as an individual and depending on someone else to make you feel good enough. Telling yourself you don't need anyone else is, likewise, futile as it means you are equally unable to manage your feelings.

Usually, people who rely on others to validate their self-worth can become overwhelmed with emotion whenever they are disappointed. As a result, arguments can readily occur and quickly escalate. However, being in connection with someone else requires you to cope with these feelings of disappointment and vulnerability. The reality is that not coping with them yourself makes you feel even more disappointed and vulnerable. That doesn't mean you should hide feelings or that you can't ask for help to manage them; just that you acknowledge them and accept that you have responsibility for them. This way you will have genuine control. It isn't easy, but acquiring the skills to become more responsible for your own feelings of self-esteem will improve your life all round as well as your sex life and relationship.

The ability to examine your motivation is very important in allowing you to understand what you want. It is all too easy once you've done this to hope or expect that your partner will find a way to meet your needs. However, this apparently easy way out actually causes complications, as neither of you probably feels in control of what is happening. Instead of this, you could think about what you could do to meet your own needs. For instance, if you feel you need space when you get in from work, but your partner wants to chat, you may be dealing with this by either putting up with the chatter or going off alone and leaving your partner to stew. A more helpful approach would be to explain to your partner that if you take time for a gear change when you get home you will be more available for a proper chat afterwards. This way both your needs are met. Similarly, if your sexual needs cause you embarrassment, explain this and maybe show rather than tell your partner what you like if this feels more comfortable. Working out what you can do for yourself and what you need help with is the key to taking control. Expecting your partner to guess is likely to leave you both feeling disappointed.

It isn't just the obvious outward things which affect self-image. How we perceive our relationships in private is also reflected in the way we see ourselves. Sometimes, even when you are alone with your partner you may feel as though other people know and judge your behaviour and what it says about you. Though this is not a fully conscious process, we make judgements as to what our private behaviour says about us. As a result we sometimes don't want others to know about behaviours we think would reflect badly on us or make others respect us less. For instance, if a man has the idea that he needs to be very sexually active, able and adventurous to be considered masculine, he may see his partner's lack of interest in sex as reflecting badly on his self-image and pester her for sex as a result.

If you have worked through the exercises and considered the ideas in this chapter, you may now be feeling more aware of ways to look after yourself as well as to nurture your relationship. A major first step is to acknowledge that it takes effort and thought to work out the reasons for our own motivations and behaviour, let alone the motivations of our partner. It is much harder to see others' point of view when we are consumed by our own confusing emotions. However, working out our own feelings and needs helps us determine what we can do to meet them and when we need to ask for help. This may take some courage but is more effective than hoping your partner can guess what you are thinking and fix things for you.

This chapter has shown that a common reason for awkwardness is fear of getting things wrong. This is never more evident than in terms of sexual performance, where we all take risks which can affect both our relationship and our self-image, as Chapter Six explains.

Chapter Six
Sexual Performance

Being 'good enough in bed' is a preoccupation of many people, yet few have a definite idea of what 'good enough' means. What is sexual dynamite for one person could be the excitement equivalent of watching paint dry for another. This is especially the case for women, whose sexual needs may vary not just from woman to woman, or from time to time, but from moment to moment.

Performance is rarely what is most important about the sexual experience and worrying about performance can spoil it. Being in the moment allows you to appreciate the closeness you feel during sex with your partner. This helps you to work together at achieving mutual sexual satisfaction. Indeed, sexual satisfaction ultimately relies on each partner's ability to take responsibility for their own arousal and orgasm. Partners aren't mind readers and need help to offer each other the pleasure they both seek.

Men's particular concern is often that they will ejaculate early or not be able to achieve or maintain an erection. However, worrying about this can make it happen – in any case, women's sexual satisfaction is unlikely to be achieved through intercourse alone. A fixation with the penis can mean overlooking the sensual and erotic aspects of lovemaking which create a really special experience.

AROUSING WOMEN

The difference in women's sexual response can lead some partners to question their technique. So many factors influence women's responsiveness that they may be extremely quick to arouse to orgasm(s) on some occasions and very slow at other times.

Stimulation of the clitoris is what usually leads to women's orgasms, but how soon to begin clitoral touch varies. Most women like to be at least a little aroused before clitoral stimulation begins. Moreover, prolonged clitoral stimulation can become uncomfortable and variation in pressure or position may be needed on different occasions or even from one minute to the next. For men who have developed a reliable technique for self-stimulation, this can be bewildering – why do women keep wanting to alter pressure, have a different spot touched, use a different technique? Understandably, men can feel hurt when their partners ask them to change what they just seemed to be doing successfully.

Unlike men, women don't experience a 'point of inevitability' – when orgasm is unavoidable – so stimulation may need to continue as the orgasm begins and even beyond, or the woman's arousal can abruptly stop. Those women who like to have multiple orgasms may want stimulation to continue indefinitely or require a different kind of stimulation to climax again. As this is such an individual experience, which can vary from one occasion to the next, it is understandable that getting it right can cause anxiety.

VAGINAL ORGASM

Another issue affecting many couples is the idea that women should orgasm during intercourse and that their partner should be responsible for their orgasm. Sometimes, partners feel guilty if the woman doesn't climax and the woman feels under pressure to orgasm to make her partner feel good. Despite this, many couples don't talk about their lovemaking or what they could do to enhance it. In particular, women are often reluctant to ask partners for more, or any, clitoral stimulation in case it makes the partner feel inadequate. Instead, they may fake orgasm to please their partner. Ironically, studies also show that many women are more interested in feeling close and connected when they make love than in attaining an orgasm every time. However, the pressure on both of the couple to achieve the climax may inhibit their feelings of closeness and connection.

MISGUIDED EXPECTATIONS

When the sex researchers William Masters and Virginia Johnson developed their sex-therapy programme back in the 1960s and 1970s, much of their work was focused on educating couples about their bodies and sexual functioning. The sexual revolution that their work significantly contributed to helped transform the availability of both formal and informal sexual information so that it is now often taken for granted that we all understand sex. However, though we may be more knowledgeable about some body parts and have expectations of sexual pleasure, many of us still have unrealistic or misguided expectations and ideas. These may contribute to the development of sexual problems, to dissatisfaction with sex or to concern about doing it properly or getting it right. This is particularly challenging if we believe everyone else seems to be managing well and enjoying a range of sexual activities.

It is not only the way we behave which bothers many of us but also the way our bodies behave. It is quite usual to have some fears that our bodies will let us down or to be worried about whether our bodily functions and bodies are 'normal', as the section on body knowledge demonstrates (see page 98). Mild concern can become a preoccupation, however, so that we start observing our own performance during sex, a phenomenon known as 'spectatoring'.

Spectatoring is associated with high anxiety and anticipation of failure. You may be very sensitive to your partner's opinion and on the lookout for criticism, which you may readily perceive. Spectatoring itself causes the anticipated problems because it is impossible to relax and be in the moment when you are watching yourself or looking for hitches.

When performance anxiety or sex avoidance starts to get the better of you, it can be very helpful to formally ban sex and start again, getting used to one another's bodies using sensual touch. It can also be very helpful if the 'threat' of sex is preventing you from enjoying any touch at all.

Simply agreeing that sex is off the agenda for a period of time will allow you to relax and appreciate kisses and cuddles without worrying about what comes next. This is often so enjoyable that couples are keen to break the sex ban and resume intercourse early. However, it is worth sticking with it, as you will probably emerge from the period of sexual embargo with a completely different, more positive attitude to touch and even to your relationship overall. Starting from scratch allows you to break bad habits, learn about your bodies and embrace strategies which enable you to deal with problems as they arise. Discovering how to be 'in the moment' also helps banish performance fears and helps you to relax.

TOUCHING EXERCISES

If you wanted to take this a step further, you could try introducing some touching exercises to help you reconnect. Masters and Johnson called these 'sensate focus exercises' and they are still 'prescribed' by psychosexual therapists as they can have such a dramatic effect on a couple's feelings of connection and sensual awareness. The idea is to explore each other's bodies without attempting arousal or any sort of sexual effect.

This is not an activity to rush or treat lightly. To make it really effective, it is worth making it special. You need sufficient time and privacy and a warm, safe room where you both feel comfortable. You might want to add soft lighting, gentle music and candles, joss sticks or warm aromatherapy oils. You will probably enjoy having a bath or shower first so that you feel relaxed and have no worries about hygiene.

If you find naked touch embarrassing, or are self-conscious about your body, you might want to begin by just touching the face and arms, or perhaps beginning with the hand-touching exercise on page 15. Alternatively, you could wear a vest or bra and pants, which will also help you to avoid obviously sexual areas such as breasts, buttocks and genitals. Ideally, though, you will be naked and lie down together with eyes open. Talking, as well as sex, is discouraged so that you can focus on the activity completely.

Body exploration

Once you are comfortable, take turns to explore each other's bodies, moving one another whichever way you wish and touching in whatever way you choose. Avoid touching breasts, buttocks or genitals – this is an exercise to explore the areas of the body which are usually neglected. You may, for instance, discover that you love to kiss the back of your partner's neck, caress their elbows or rest your head on their tummy or chest and smell their familiar scent. You can use different pressure and touch with fingertips or your whole hand, use only one hand or both. You can gently puff or blow; you can even use your lips and tongue – but remember you are not intending to arouse. This exploration is meant to please *you*, not to arouse your partner.

This is not the same as massage, where you are working beyond the surface skin, deep into the muscle below. With this exercise, you are concentrating only on the skin, so touch needs to be either light or firm, but gentle. For instance, use the flat of your hand or your fingertips to avoid pinching, kneading or grabbing.

It is a good idea to repeat the full exercise on a few occasions so that you become really comfortable with it. To begin with, you may feel self-conscious, giggly or bored. It often takes more than one attempt to really focus and get the most from it. As you become familiar with the exercise, you can add oil, moisturiser or talc, or experiment with different textures, such as feathers, scarves, cotton wool or washcloths. When you are on the receiving end, notice how these feel on different parts of your body, which you most enjoy using and which you most like to be used to touch you. You may enjoy surprising one another with different items, though it isn't helpful to be too competitive about this.

After the exercise

Make sure that you don't rush off after the exercise. Spend some time resting and cuddling together and allowing yourselves to feel connected. Discussing the exercise later can be very helpful so long as you are positive. Give full consideration to the experience and what you may say about it before you have a conversation about what happened. Most importantly, this should not be an opportunity for criticism.

It may initially be more helpful to talk about what you liked doing to your partner rather than what it was like being touched. It can be beneficial to you to think first about whether anything made you feel self-conscious or uncomfortable. Feeling awkward is more likely to lead us to make blaming statements to our partners, to try to relieve our own discomfort. If you can identify and manage uncomfortable feelings before speaking to your partner about them, you may have a more honest and appreciative conversation.

Thinking about the exercise on your own before discussing what happened may also help you to identify your needs and think about how you can go about meeting them. It may be that you discover you absolutely love having your head stroked or that you enjoy kissing your partner's shoulders. Perhaps it is their response you love, or maybe you just enjoy the sensation and scent of their skin. As your familiarity with the exercise grows, you may come to see these touching exercises as a great form of communication, allowing you to show your partner your interest, love and, later, your desire.

Slowing things down and getting to know each other's bodies gives you space and time for discovery and learning, about yourself and your partner. You may find that you do feel aroused by the sensate focus exercises, and that's okay. Notice this if it happens, and enjoy it, but don't act on it. Don't be competitive about who was aroused or blame one another either for your arousal or lack of sexual feelings. The sensate focus exercises are all about gentle discovery, so if you go into them with a different agenda they will inevitably be sabotaged. Realistically, it can take a few attempts to leave your agenda in the bathroom, so you may need to be patient. Often, one partner finds this easier than the other. Eventually, you will learn to be in the moment – and it may be a moment you hope will last forever.

Sensual discovery

Once you feel completely comfortable with the exercises, you could begin to incorporate exploration of breasts, buttocks and genitals – but, once again, this is not meant to be about arousal. It will be interesting to reflect on the differences in this and the previous sensate focus exercises. You may find the idea of genital touching more threatening or find yourself having expectations of arousal or disappointment which you hadn't previously realised are part of your experience when you make love.

If this is too much, go back to the earlier non-arousal exercises for a while and introduce the other body parts more gradually, perhaps beginning with just buttocks. Notice whether you have any aversion to being touched or looked at in particular places or whether there is anywhere you don't like touching your partner. Can you think why this might be? These slow exploratory exercises give you the space to take apart your sensual expectations and experience piece by piece so that you know yourself much better, as well as making a greater connection with your partner.

If you manage to become comfortable with non-arousal genital touch, you may find yourself becoming aroused. It is fine if you don't – arousal is not the intention of the exercises – but notice whether this is because you push the arousal away as it begins or whether there are aspects of the exercises that you really don't like. Treat the exercises as experimental and all you will do is learn. There is no right or wrong response to them.

Attempting arousal

If you feel ready, you could move gingerly to attempt arousal. You may wish to do this in stages, perhaps going back to non-genital touch but enjoying deep kissing and full body contact. If you do attempt arousal, do not expect it to end in orgasm. In fact, the more you allow arousal without orgasm, the more you will become confident about your body's response and look forward to exploring it further.

You can build up the amount of erotic touch as you feel comfortable with it. To begin with, keep this exploratory and then gradually start to discuss what you enjoy about the exercises. It is probably best initially to save this until afterwards. The time may come when you would like to guide your partner's hand or ask them to do something you enjoy. However, don't demand anything you know your partner probably won't like; this is not an excuse to pester for an activity that your partner has previously refused. Doing so could destroy the trust which has been built between you. If your partner does want to try something they have previously refused, they can let you know.

Incidentally, you should agree in advance that exercises can be stopped if necessary and that you will each let the other know if anything they are doing actually hurts. You can't know in advance how you will feel or how your touch will be received, so if something feels uncomfortable this is good to know so that you can find ways to work round this. Stopping is not always because of discomfort; sometimes it is possible to feel so overwhelmed by the warmth and love that has developed between you that you are too moved to continue.

Arousal to orgasm

The erotic touch stages are just as experimental as the earlier ones. The idea is not to just go back to the way you used to make love but to develop new and different approaches, which make the whole experience of lovemaking into an endless journey of discovery. If one of you orgasms and the other doesn't, so be it.

When you feel confident in the exercises, you may want to try deliberately arousing each other to orgasm. Once you feel this is working successfully, the exercises will transition into lovemaking with mutual pleasure expected and achieved at least some of the time. Don't rush to incorporate penetration. When you are ready, introduce it as part of your repertoire, but don't make it the main focus or you will lose out on all the sensual learning and closeness you have worked at.

If you have any difficulty, or problems achieving erection, orgasm or penetration, you may wish to consider psychosexual therapy (also see Chapter Twelve pages 182–190). The therapist will be able to guide you through a tailor-made programme, based on a thorough history, which will address any functional difficulties as well as developing your overall sexual experience. Of course, you don't need to try the sensate focus exercises before attending therapy. It can be very reassuring to have support and guidance from the beginning.

Mindfulness

Either way, you and your partner can both benefit from familiarity with mindfulness and thinking exercises to get the most out of the sensate focus experience. This is helpful to keep you in the moment, whether you are doing the touching or receiving touch. Mindfulness helps you to feel present and focused and to manage distractions with simple exercises based on meditation which help you to focus on the here and now. You could begin by practising mindfulness in the bath before your sensate focus exercises. You may enjoy a bath or shower, but how often do you really notice and appreciate the feeling and temperature of the water, the steam, your body's response? Noticing can help you to form a habit of appreciating what is happening in the here and now. You will develop real sensual awareness and pleasure in sensual touch, so that you are more able to enjoy all experiences, including sex.

An outdoor mindfulness exercise is included on page 43. Below is an indoor mindfulness exercise that is best attempted in sections, which build on each other. Starting with the breathing exercises will help to calm you, and you should feel confident about these before moving on to the following stage, which helps you to relax your body and increase your awareness of touch. Again, this should be attempted several times, with the breathing, before moving on to the listening exercise and, finally, incorporating the thinking section. Practising for five minutes once or twice a day quickly allows you to feel comfortable with the exercise, to incorporate it into sensate focus and, ultimately, into your lovemaking.

EXERCISE: INDOOR MINDFULNESS

1. Breathing

➤ Sit or lie down somewhere comfortable and where you won't be disturbed.

➤ Close your eyes and allow yourself to concentrate on your breathing.

➤ Be aware of breathing in deeply; as you breathe out, let your body relax with the breath.

➤ As your breathing begins to slow down, allow yourself to develop a rhythm – breathing in ... and out ... in ... and out ...

2. Touch

➤ Be aware of your thighs and back touching the chair or your head, back and legs touching the bed. Notice what that feels like.

➤ Next, focus on your hands and what they are touching. Notice the textures your fingers are experiencing.
Let your focus move to different parts of your body, becoming aware of the variety of physical sensations you find there. Notice any discomfort, aches or pain. If possible, avoid focusing on any discomfort; describe the feelings to yourself and then allow them to drift away.

3. Sound

➤ Once you have become confident with the breathing and touch exercises, focus your attention on sounds.

➤ Notice different sounds, both inside and outside the room.

➤ Try to identify them, then let these thoughts go.

4. Thinking

➤ Now allow yourself to be aware again of your feet on the floor or your back on the bed.

> ➤ Notice the feeling of the ground beneath your feet or the mattress supporting your body.
> ➤ Be aware of your relationship with your surroundings, of your perceptions, of the air around you, the smells, the sounds and the sensations.
> ➤ This time if any thoughts or feelings bother you, imagine they are no more than puffs of smoke floating into the distance.
> ➤ Once they have gone, concentrate again on all that is around you, noticing your breathing, the physical sensations, the sounds and the smells ... Relax.

Unwanted thoughts

The hardest part of the mindfulness exercise is often managing unwanted thoughts and feelings which can pop up. It doesn't take much imagination to appreciate that thoughts and feelings can emerge to interfere with your sexual experiences too. Anxiety can appear from nowhere; it may not even be recognised as anxiety, yet it can cause stress, which leads to performance difficulty. For instance, you may be becoming nicely relaxed and then find yourself imagining what will happen if your erection lets you down. Worrying about it then becomes a passion killer, which does, indeed, affect your erection. Sometimes you may not be aware of thoughts but feel an increasing sense of nervousness that seems to have appeared out of the blue.

A problem for many people is that they are unable to separate their thinking from their feelings, and they can't separate feelings from thoughts. Consequently, the beginnings of a bodily sensation associated with anxiety, anger, resentment, love, whatever, is acted on immediately without any checking of what the feeling is about. Spending more time thinking, rather than reacting, can help to sort out what is the most helpful and appropriate response. Using the mindfulness exercises regularly can help you to avoid an impulse reaction and help you to stay calm and examine what is happening in the moment.

Checking out what you think you understand with your partner is then possible. For instance, during lovemaking you may start to notice bodily anxiety and, thinking about this, decide that you are becoming worried that your partner isn't very aroused. Trying harder to arouse them, giving up, becoming preoccupied with the idea that you aren't a good enough lover or blaming your partner are common knee-jerk reactions. Alternatively, you could assess the evidence for your concerns and, if they really seem valid, ask your partner how they are feeling, how the lovemaking is going or whether they would like you to do anything differently. If questions seem out of place, maybe you could just ask them to guide your hand.

Without some reflection, many of us just assume our concerns are correct and respond without thinking the situation through, even though the assumption may be very mistaken. For example, some people become quiet and still when they are concentrating on their orgasm and this can easily be construed as losing interest – when nothing is further from the truth.

It may be appropriate to wait until after lovemaking to investigate whether your anxious feeling was correct. You might decide that blurting out fretful demands for reassurance will spoil the mood. If that's the case, and there is a mood to spoil, maybe there isn't any problem after all. In this case, familiarity with mindfulness will help you to let the anxiety pass so you can concentrate fully on lovemaking. Nonetheless, it is certainly worth discussing what happened afterwards so you can make a plan to see how you would both like to handle such situations in future.

It is often possible to identify what triggers anxiety, which is particularly useful when this is related to sexual performance. There may be a tangible thought caused by having a lot on your mind or by caring very much about getting something right. Alternatively, there may just be a triggering word or event which releases anxiety in you. Repeating the exercise above will help you to identify thoughts and triggers so you can plan with your partner how to deal with anxious feelings when they occur. It is easy to panic, so you may need to develop some self-talk which helps to calm you and/or ask your partner for hugs or reassurance when you start to feel overwhelmed by unpleasant thoughts or feelings.

Anxiety associated with arousal may be linked to a previous unpleasant experience which has been pushed to the back of your memory, with the expectation that the arousal will lead nowhere anyway or with a feeling that it is wrong or dirty. Very often, arousal just generates fears that you aren't a good-enough lover. These thoughts can all be challenged, with or without help from your partner. Once you realise that managing problem thoughts and feelings by avoiding them isn't really managing them at all, you will be in a much better position to allow yourself to become aroused and see what happens then. The exercises allow you to experiment with different ways of thinking and behaving, whereas avoidance just closes down all opportunities to find solutions.

This chapter has contained a number of strategies and ideas to help banish performance anxiety and increase your sensual awareness. The next section looks at external factors in your life which may help or hinder your sexual expression and experience.

Part Three
Overcoming Sexual Challenges

Chapter Seven
Body Knowledge

Concern about how our bodies look, perform, feel and smell can easily inhibit sexual desire. Insecurity and self-consciousness don't encourage sexual behaviour and many people who avoid sex do so just because they feel awkward or anxious about their bodies. This isn't necessarily about eating disorders or body dysmorphia; this is about everyday self-consciousness and insecurity.

You may have been with your partner for years and never been able to shake off negative feelings about your body. Or they may develop after having a baby, around the menopause or over time. If this sounds like you, keep remembering that your partner is making love to all of you, not just your spare tyre. Attraction over time is not just about looks; it is all about your shared experiences and the life you have created together.

Indeed, partners often don't know how to deal with self-consciousness. Teasing about body concerns may be aimed to lighten distress, but this can backfire if the teasing comes across as critical or uncaring. Blanket reassurance is often unhelpful, however, as it rarely seems genuine. Telling your partner not to be silly because you can't see a problem is also unlikely to alleviate their distress as it disqualifies their feelings.

Instead, be sensitive to what helps your partner feel less self-conscious when you make love. If it makes them feel better to do something like keeping the lights low or off, or making love partially clothed, try not to discourage this or tease them about it. Patience and understanding is much more effective than irritation in helping one another to relax and forget about body concerns.

BREASTS

Understanding how your body functions can be very reassuring in itself, as many of us feel different and assume we are alone in this. For instance, you – like many of us – may worry unnecessarily about subtleties of breast shape, colour and size which may not be noticeable to anyone else. Reassurance that breasts come in all shapes and sizes, with a range of difference in the appearance of nipples too, is little help when the ones we actually see are all airbrushed to perfection. This makes the way they are naturally seem 'wrong'. It can be a surprise too to discover that they change in response to hormones. For instance, your partner may love the post-pregnancy size and shape of your breasts, while you may dislike their heaviness or the network of veins which can appear in breastfeeding mums. Alternatively, you may delight in them as evidence that your body is behaving as it should, while your partner is a little intimidated by their new function.

THE VAGINA

As a result of the availability of pornography, many boys and girls get their ideas about how their bodies should look from the often highly unrealistic appearance of porn actors and glamour models. As if worrying about breasts wasn't enough, many women are ashamed of their genitals, believing they are ugly. If you are convinced that your own vulva is particularly unsightly, this will almost certainly prevent you from being able to relax when you are being touched. Avoiding oral sex, for instance, is a common consequence of embarrassment about genital appearance or odour.

The vulva

Vulvas do have differences, but there is no reason why one should be assumed to be prettier than another. It is a useful exercise to squat down with a mirror to have a look at your own. The outer lips of the vagina, the labia majora, need to be separated and held apart to see your vulva properly. The vagina itself is found at the bottom of the vulva, above the perineum, which is the area between the genitals and anus. You may be able to see the remains of your hymen at the vaginal opening. The urethral opening, from which you wee, can be found above the vagina. This area is surrounded and protected by the inner lips, the labia minora. They are separated at the top by the clitoris, the structure whose only function is to produce sexual pleasure.

The clitoris

The clitoris is a large organ, only a tiny part of which is visible on the surface of the body as a small structure positioned inside the vulva, above the urethra. The clitoris has a small hood, which can be retracted; this withdraws a little during arousal and as you get older, exposing the clitoral head. The main body of the clitoris, known as the 'clitoral complex', is buried internally behind the genitals, extending on either side of the labia majora.

It is stimulation of the clitoris which results in orgasm. Stimulation can be direct or indirect, and what feels pleasurable can change from moment to moment. Some women enjoy intense pressure directly to the clitoris, such as rubbing with the fingers, while others prefer less direct and gentler touch. Dry rubbing can be painful, so some women especially enjoy clitoral touch with the lips and tongue. The type of touch and pressure required may vary a great deal in a single episode of lovemaking or may depend on level of arousal, lubrication and time of the month. If the vulval area is very dry, rubbing can make it sore, particularly after the menopause, when you are breastfeeding or while taking the contraceptive pill. Lubrication sometimes collects just inside the vaginal entrance and it may be possible to scoop this out to moisten the clitoris or use a water-based lubricant.

Familiarity with your own sexual response will help you to guide your partner when you make love. Exploring, touching and stimulating your vulva and clitoris while you watch in a mirror will show you how changes occur as you become aroused. In particular, the genitals may become darker as blood flow to the area increases. They may be significantly darker during pregnancy too due to hormonal changes and the increased blood flow. If you climax, you may be able to see the rhythmic contractions of the vagina.

Labia

The labia majora do not always enclose the labia minora, which are large enough to protrude in many women. These inner lips vary tremendously in size, colour and appearance. They may not even be the same size and shape in the same woman. For example, one may hang raggedly while the other is tucked neatly inside the labia majora. Some men and women make unfavourable comparisons with the perfect vulvas they are used to from porn. In the past, such harmful comparisons did not occur with anything like as much frequency. These comparisons have resulted in some women resorting to surgery in order to 'tidy' their labia.

It is a shame that all couples can't enjoy exploring their bodies together and accepting what they find. After all, it is not possible that genitals have only become 'deformed' recently. Corrective surgery was considerably less common before the internet made porn so widely viewed. Certainly, no one should feel pressured into making any changes to their body. Mature relationships are all about discovering and delighting in one another without an agenda.

The cervix

Looking at the vulva, it may be hard to imagine what lies behind or that the vagina could accommodate anything the size of a penis – or a baby. Yet the vagina is very elastic, stretching in response to arousal. It actually becomes wider and longer, as the position of the womb also changes during orgasm, moving up and tilting back slightly. This somewhat retracts the neck of the womb, the cervix, which normally protrudes into the top of the vagina. During childbirth the cervix retracts completely and opens to allow the baby passage into the vagina.

Some women enjoy deep penetration of the vagina so that the penis touches the cervix. Side-by-side or rear-entry intercourse shortens the vagina to make cervical touch more likely, or the depth of penetration can be controlled with the recipient on top. Some women also enjoy gentle manual stimulation of the cervix, though this needs to be done carefully to avoid scratching or bruising.

Vaginal odour

Vaginal odour is another cause of shame and body-image issues for many women, even when their partner isn't bothered by it or positively likes it. A strong musky smell is produced by secretions from the Bartholin's glands, pea-sized structures which are found on either side of the vagina within the labia majora. Production of secretions increases during sexual arousal and provides a very small amount of lubrication at the very opening to the vagina. Most of the lubrication in the vagina comes from the vaginal walls themselves and from the cervix. This is present all the time, to prevent the vaginal walls from sticking together, but is much increased during arousal. So it is thought that the Bartholin's secretion is more a vehicle for the odour, which is intended to be sexually alluring, rather than to provide much lubrication. The overall lubrication which is produced during arousal reaches a certain point and then ceases. Some women reach this stage quickly and others take longer, so there is no point in trying to suppress arousal because you don't like the amount of lubrication; it may already have stopped.

It cannot be emphasised enough that the characteristic musky odour and vaginal secretions are completely normal; it is not a good idea to scrub, douche or use chemicals to get rid of the smell. Not only will it not work but you may remove healthy bacteria which help to protect the vagina and prevent infection. Washing once or twice a day with soap and water is sufficient. Yeast infections, such as thrush, occur when healthy bacteria are compromised, by over-washing or use of antibiotics, for example.

Vaginal discharge

Vaginal secretions also affect body image, worrying some women, perhaps because they are less present before puberty and so seem unusual when they begin. There is often a brownish or cream-coloured discharge after a period, which becomes clearer as the month progresses. By the time of ovulation at mid-month the discharge has become transparent and can be almost watery. If you are able to scoop some up and stretch it between your fingers, you will see that it is highly elastic at this time and does not break when stretched. This is the most fertile mucus and sometimes only lasts for a few hours, but it can be extremely copious, causing noticeable wetness. This mucus facilitates the movement of sperm, so is essential for fertility and does not occur if you use hormonal contraceptives. Later in the month, following ovulation, the mucus becomes sticky, thicker and whiter. It may appear as a flaky stain on the underwear as menstruation draws nearer.

Infection may be indicated if the mucus is grey, very thick and creamy, yellow or green, and especially if it has a different or fishy odour. Some men and women report a fishy smell at orgasm or after sex, which can indicate a chronic infection. All potential infections should be medically checked. An untreated infection can lead to pelvic inflammatory disease, which can threaten fertility the longer it is left.

Some women experience a kind of ejaculation from the Skene's glands, which are located near to the urethra. These glands produce a fluid similar to that from the male prostate gland. Some women, or their partners, confuse this with urine and so may even try to avoid orgasm, as they find this so embarrassing. Even though all women don't seem to have Skene's glands, and don't ejaculate, ejaculation is normal if you do. You could be considered very lucky, as stimulation of these glands is said to cause different and more intense orgasm. There is more about female ejaculation and the Skene's glands on page 230.

PENIS SIZE

Men also worry about their appearance, especially their weight, hair, man boobs and – most of all, perhaps – the look of their penis. Just like the vulva and breasts, the penis comes in a variety of shapes and sizes, and there is no perfect organ to aspire to. On average, the penis is five or six inches long when erect and wouldn't be considered unusually small unless it measured less than three inches. The smaller the penis when flaccid, the larger it usually becomes when erect. Studies have shown that it is common for men to worry about the appearance of their penis even when they have been reassured it is absolutely normal.

Since intercourse alone is rarely the most effective way to cause orgasm in women, and men who have sex with men can orgasm through both receptive and penetrative sex, penis *size* is fairly irrelevant. However, reality doesn't have much influence when it comes to body concerns. Myths about the benefits of large penises are persistent and the large men in porn don't do much to reassure the majority who are more normally endowed. Instead of worrying about what your penis isn't, do think about what it *can* do and the pleasure it gives you.

MALE GENITALIA

The most sensitive area of the penis is the helmet-like head or 'glans' which is covered by the foreskin if not circumcised. Inside, the 'shaft', or body, of the penis contains erectile tissue which becomes engorged with blood during arousal, leading to erection. Below the penis, the sack of skin known as the scrotum contains two testicles, which are responsible for the manufacture and storage of sperm. Before ejaculation, a first phase of contractions transports the sperm along a tube called the vas deferens, where they become mixed with secretions from the prostate and seminal vesicles. They then enter the urethra from where they are expelled with the stronger rhythmic contractions of ejaculation.

The tiny Cowper's gland secretes a clear fluid during arousal which lubricates the urethra to facilitate transportation of the sperm. This can be barely noticeable or may appear in copious amounts in some men. This fluid, referred to as 'pre-ejaculate' or 'pre-cum', can contain some sperm, so contraceptive precautions may be necessary from an early stage in lovemaking if there is a great deal of pre-cum.

It is normal for testicles to be different sizes and to hang differently, and it is important for all men to know the particular features of their genitals in case any untoward changes occur. Just as women check their breasts regularly, it is important that men become familiar with their testicles so that you are able to notice any changes right away. Rolling them between your thumbs and forefingers, you should be able to detect lumps and thickenings which may need medical attention.

However, looking down at your penis and scrotum means that you never really see them properly. Using both a full-length mirror and a small mirror held underneath your genitals allows a better view of your penis, testicles, perineum and anal area. Have a good look, noticing the different textures and appearance of the skin from different angles. If you stimulate yourself at the same time, you may notice that your testicles move up towards the body as you become more aroused, changing from their smooth, loose appearance and becoming tenser and more wrinkled. Squatting or sitting with your legs apart, and using a hand mirror, can also help you to see and touch the area, noting what you enjoy. Your own touch may be very different from your partner's; you may even prefer the way you touch yourself. However, in masturbation you may have been focusing entirely on your penis and what it takes to orgasm. Experimentation may help you discover that the testicles, perineum and anal area can be exquisitely sensitive too.

This chapter has looked at some of the ways concern and lack of knowledge can affect us and our relationship. The following chapter also looks at the way relationships can be affected by one partner's behaviour and feelings, but in this case they involve matters which may be deliberately hidden from partners. As we shall see, sexual secrets can have profound effects on both the individual and the relationship, though many relationships survive them very well.

Chapter Eight
Sexual Secrets

Sexual secrets can be defined as anything sexually related which is kept hidden. These are not the kind of secrets which are shared between partners within a couple relationship, but secrets which may be kept from partners and the outside world. Where there is shame about it, sometimes the partner with the secret won't even admit it to themselves. Shame often prevents both the individual partner and the couple from seeking help, making the secret even more pernicious and threatening to the relationship.

Sometimes, however, the secret is more embarrassing than threatening. When one partner keeps a sexual preference secret from the other, it is usually either because they don't think the partner would want to join in or they are embarrassed about it.

MASTURBATION

Masturbation is a sexual secret which isn't really a secret at all. Whether or not they acknowledge or talk about it, partners often assume the other sometimes masturbates. However, masturbation can be denied or compulsively hidden if one or both partners feel it is some sort of betrayal. Or they may worry that there is something wrong if their partner masturbates, believing that they should only be fulfilled by sex with each other.

The difference between masturbation and partner sex, however, is like the difference between a snack and a banquet. Masturbation may be comforting or help you to relax, or it may deal with intense moments of arousal; what it doesn't usually do is provide the sense of occasion, connection or achievement which may be associated with lovemaking.

A negative attitude towards masturbation sometimes develops when someone has been in trouble for touching themselves as a child or actively told that it is wrong or damaging. However, even when they have no memories at all associated with masturbation or self-touch, many people still feel guilty about it.

Fortunately, improved sex education should convince future generations that masturbation is a natural way to experiment and learn about your body in ways that can also be very helpful to partners. As an occasional or daily practice, it can be relaxing and can cause no harm to yourself or anyone else. Some couples masturbate together; this can be both arousing and help you show each other how you enjoy being touched.

CASE EXAMPLE: PIP AND NOR

Pip was hurt when Nor told her he had masturbated after she rang him during a business trip. Nor told her about this because he thought it demonstrated how much he cared for and missed her, especially as they had been flirting over the phone and enjoying talking about what they would do together sexually when Nor got back. Nor found it difficult to understand Pip's distress; he told her he would have been flattered if she had also masturbated after the call.

Though Pip was initially shocked by this, it prompted her to talk to a couple of close friends about the idea of masturbation in committed relationships. She was surprised to find they knew about their partners masturbating and occasionally did so themselves. Meanwhile, Nor was distressed that Pip saw his masturbation as a sort of betrayal. He explained to her that missing her and finding her so attractive led to him using masturbation to comfort himself when they were apart. Pip continued to struggle with this, but was gradually able to accept that Nor's masturbation did not reflect badly on his love for her.

FETISHES

Generally speaking, a fetish can be considered anything – usually other than the human body – which, in itself, produces sexual arousal. Commonly, this can be rubber, especially rubber clothing, items of underwear, boots or high heels. However, fetishes can attach to anything with an erotic association. Sometimes, the individual likes to wear the item themselves or encourages their partner to wear it, which may be considered as an occasional and completely acceptable variant to lovemaking. For instance, you may like to see your partner dressed in frilly underwear or only become properly aroused if you or your partner wears a particular scent.

Rarely do fetishes involve more than a strong desire to include some item or idea in fantasy, lovemaking or masturbation. On their own, individuals with a fetish may want to hold the object(s), rub themselves against it, kiss it, touch it, insert it, wear it, be near it. Problems usually arise when the amount of time spent focused on the object starts to interfere with everyday life or lovemaking.

Body fetishes

Some fetishes do concern the body and may involve being really turned on by something like hair, feet, the smell of sweat or even by disability or mutilation. This may present a problem for a relationship, especially if this is the only way to become aroused and/or it is unusual or distasteful to the partner. Nevertheless, there are clubs and parties where fetishes can be indulged. Some couples enjoy regular or occasional visits; others find it is impossible to manage within their relationship. Generally speaking, this is a matter for the couple to negotiate, with or without the assistance of counselling. However, pressuring your partner into sexual acts which they are uncomfortable with is not loving or fair, and may even be illegal.

As with all sexual secrets, discovery that the fetish exists needs coming to terms with before considering the fetish itself and what it means for the relationship. You may find the fetish amusing and even be able to participate or indulge it; you may find it totally abhorrent; or you may have mixed feelings which you find difficult or confusing. Your concern may be that the fetish could lead to problems for your partner.

When fetishes are indulged outside of informed adult consent, they almost always become problematic and can involve offending. For instance, stealing underwear from clothes lines is joked about in relation to fetishes, but it does sometimes happen. More seriously, some people touch or follow members of the public who are wearing the object they like or look the way they like; for instance, their interest may be long hair, which they can't resist touching. In such cases, it really is time to seek professional help to confine interests to non-offending means of expression.

In some couples, one partner is tolerant of, or turns a blind eye towards, the other's fetish. Some partners feel able to participate and others can't continue with the relationship unless the fetish stops. Initial responses on either side may not be your reaction given more time to think things over, and possibly more information. Some partners find confiding in friends is helpful. Even just searching the internet to learn more may be useful.

Though you may feel a huge sense of betrayal if you have just discovered your partner has a secret fetish, it is important to remember that nothing has actually changed apart from what you know. Your partner is still the same person that you loved before you knew about the fetish. Depending on how easy you find it to talk about, you may be able to reach an agreement that suits both of you. However, couple counselling may offer a neutral space where you can work out how to go forward once the fetish has been disclosed.

TRANSVESTISM

Men who enjoy dressing as women are known as transvestites. Discovery that a partner likes to cross-dress is very common, and not always associated with sexual arousal. Where particular items of clothing do lead to arousal, transvestism is often seen as a form of fetish. For instance, some men aren't interested in passing as a woman but love wearing women's underwear. This may be during lovemaking or when they are out and about; it is their secret and this may be part of the pleasure. Some men are only interested in underwear which has been worn.

Sometimes, this is something couples are able to accommodate in their lives together. When it has been a secret, however, finding out can come as a major shock. If you cross-dress, you may be very relieved when your partner finds out and be completely frank with them about this side of yourself; you may even want to incorporate it into your life as a couple. Some partners do accept cross-dressing as a facet of the other's personality. However, not all partners can cope with the thought of cross-dressing.

Partners of transvestites

If you have just made the discovery that your partner cross-dresses, you will need time to see whether this is something you are able to come to terms with. For some partners, the behaviour itself might not be so much the issue as the idea that it has been kept secret. Because it affects how you see yourself, you may wonder if you were not sexually fulfilling enough, feeling guilty about occasions when you have turned down sex or avoided being adventurous. Or you may feel there is something wrong with you to have made such an unwise relationship choice. You may just be totally repulsed.

A common fear is that your partner may want to completely change gender. However, recent European studies suggest that the majority of transvestites are married with children and content with their male gender. Depending on the strength of the relationship to begin with, and how personally affected the partner feels, cross-dressing often *can* be successfully managed within the relationship. Some men want to keep it as exclusively their interest while others enjoy activities with their partner *en femme*. Indeed, you may be so relieved that your secret is now out in the open that you want to start incorporating it into your life together straight away. However, partners normally need time to adjust and rushing them could make them just reject the idea. In particular, *don't* be tempted to appear *en femme* in front of your partner without discussing this with them first. Take things slowly and see how you both feel as the idea sinks in. As with discovery of all sexual secrets, this is something you may decide to take to counselling.

INTERNET PORNOGRAPHY

How prepared couples are to share their sexual interests varies a great deal. The use of erotica and pornography is an issue which provokes great controversy. Some people have ethical or moral objections to pornography, objections to some types of pornography or only find it acceptable when associated with couple arousal. Nevertheless, it is now so widespread and available that, for some individuals, its use has become as routine as a nightcap in providing a way to relax and unwind.

An orgasm stabilises the body, returning it to a calm state. It is understandable, then, to use sex to relax at times when you are jangling with stress. Internet porn can provide a quick and easy way to help you achieve that. Unfortunately, however, it can become a problem if it starts to be the only way you can become aroused or deal with stress, or if you feel you will be stressed if you don't use it. Relate counsellors are increasingly seeing problems with relationships and sexual functioning that are associated with the use of internet porn. This isn't about having a healthy sexual appetite or multiple partners but about a compulsion to keep returning to the activity which is causing them problems.

CASE EXAMPLE: ALAN AND RUTH

Alan had a busy management job and often worked long hours. He tried to be home before the children went to bed and was usually able to have dinner with his partner, Ruth, but often needed to spend an hour or so finishing paperwork in the evening. He always left for work before the rest of the family got up in the morning.

One night, while he was working on a particularly difficult project, he started surfing the computer to look at porn sites. He spent an hour or so exploring, and masturbating on and off. After he had ejaculated, he felt much better and spent another 90 minutes finishing his work. He slept well that night.

His use of internet porn became a habit on most days. He started to see it as a way of helping him work and also of getting 'me time' away from the stress of work and family. He began watching TV with Ruth after dinner and starting work quite late while she was getting ready for bed. He would work for a while and then reward himself by going on porn sites, though he found it increasingly difficult to find material that was really exciting. He was staying up later and later, searching.

He started to think about the porn sites during the day at work and feel resentful that he didn't have more time to visit them. Sometimes he even looked at them during the day. He started coming home later, as he would either need to stay on at work to complete tasks he had neglected or call at a pub to look at the sites on his phone while he had a pint. He often had to work at the weekend to make up for what he hadn't done during the week.

Initially, Ruth had noticed that Alan's new regime made him seem less stressed. She was thrilled that he wanted to spend time with her in the evening though she was a bit concerned at how late he had to work as a result. She sometimes suggested he skip TV and come to bed with her. Gradually, she became concerned. They hadn't made love for nearly a year and this was starting to worry her. Indeed, the last time they tried, Alan had not been able to climax. There were few nights now when Alan wasn't on the computer, even at the weekend, and he was often too tired to join in with family life. He hardly ever saw the children. That he was becoming addicted to internet porn never even crossed Ruth's mind until she came downstairs for breakfast one Sunday morning and found Alan still at the computer, watching a blonde woman masturbating in front of her webcam.

This was the catalyst the couple needed to begin to take control. After an initial period of shock and anger, Ruth realised they both needed to find ways to be more supportive of each other – especially if they were to get through this difficult time. After long talks, they could both see that their strategies for dealing with their stress were actually just ways of avoiding having to cope with the challenges their lives together posed. Realising how much they had to lose, Alan joined a therapy group for people with compulsive sexual behaviours and Ruth sought support through individual counselling with Relate. Some months later, they were ready to begin couple counselling which focused on healing the lack of trust in the relationship and planning ways to avoid anything similar happening again.

Cybersex and brain changes

In addition to background and personality traits, use of the internet can accelerate difficulties because of its incredibly rapid response. Indeed, there is mounting evidence that internet use changes the brain. Combined with the effect of sexual hormones, this can make internet porn powerfully attractive, more appealing ultimately than sex with a partner. This is because the 'quick fix' associated with internet use makes it more difficult to enjoy sex when it involves the effort of engaging with another person. Indeed, erectile problems may emerge or you may find it takes much longer to orgasm with a partner, if you can manage it at all (see also pages 162 and 171).

It is also possible that, in some individuals, the body starts to rely on the pleasure associated with release of the neurochemical dopamine. Dopamine is released during pleasurable activities, including sex, and creates a kind of impulse memory which makes you want to repeat the pleasant activity. As the attachment hormone oxytocin is also released, there is a theory that you can actually start to bond with the internet activity.

Just thinking about the activity – or eventually even just about your computer – can release dopamine, so you may develop a cycle which involves a great deal of time spent thinking about and planning the behaviour as well as carrying it out. However, dopamine levels plummet after orgasm, which may leave you feeling irritable, ashamed and empty. You need another fix to take away that feeling.

Once this cycle has evolved, you will probably need professional help to break it and to stay away from it. Because internet use is so solitary, there is rarely anyone to intervene and help with this if you continue to go it alone. Some people are able to make a real effort to wean themselves off internet porn by filling their time with other activities and looking forward to non-porn treats, but there is no doubt this is difficult to do by yourself. Telling someone else may mean you will get some support for efforts to change and encouragement to stick at it. Finding ways to remove some of the stress from your life is an excellent start, which may be something your partner can help with.

Partners

If you have discovered that your partner is affected by compulsive sexual behaviour, you will most likely experience a wide range of responses, from disbelief to despair and from seething to sympathy, toing and froing between a desire to help and a need to punish. You may find it impossible to understand how you did not realise what was happening, or you may realise that there have been clues you missed because of your trust. It may seem as though your partner has had an affair even though no sex with anyone else has ever taken place. It is likely that you will feel hurt that porn appears preferable to sex with you and wonder what this means for your relationship. A sense of betrayal is very common, more so if the behaviour has involved paying for porn, which can sometimes involve a considerable financial outlay.

Because the satisfaction derived from porn diminishes with exposure, it is possible that more exciting or satisfying experiences may need to be sought to elicit the same response. This may mean watching more and more violent or unusual sex as tolerance increases. Or, sometimes, this can lead surprisingly easily to actively participating in sex acts, either online or in person. As the internet gives immediate access to not just pornography but also sexual chat rooms, online sex and sex workers, it is a hop, skip and a jump from watching sex to being watched or arranging a meeting. By no means everybody who uses porn escalates their use – but the risk exists.

Women and porn

It is not just men who use the internet in this way. Research is beginning to suggest that more young women are accessing and using porn in the same way as men. Traditionally, women have been more likely than men to begin their internet compulsion by using chat rooms or social media. For instance, you may catch up with an old flame or make a friend in a chat room and begin thinking about them romantically. Before you know it, you are obsessively checking your phone for messages, agreeing to cybersex or planning a date. You may not think of this as a sexual compulsion, as you feel as though you are in a relationship, but chances are that your judgement is affected and you aren't behaving in ways that those who know you would recognise or sanction.

Sexual compulsion

Behaviour can be considered compulsive if it starts to become preoccupying; that is, if you think about it a great deal, it takes up a lot of your time and you would find it difficult to stop. When the activity starts to interfere with work or family life, it is probably time to consider getting some help to find alternative ways to relieve your stress, deal with anxiety or whatever it is that motivates you to spend so much time engaged with the behaviour.

Why some people so easily become involved to the point of compulsion is difficult to explain. Sometimes relationship problems are what start the behaviour, as it seems like a great way to escape from reality. However, many people who turn to sex for comfort or relief have a history of personal trauma which has never been resolved. Or you may be someone who, for whatever reason, just finds it very hard to calm down. For instance, you may find it difficult to regulate your feelings or comfort yourself just by self-talk or moderate use of substances or activities. You may be the sort of person who won't stop at one glass of wine but will carry on drinking until the bottle is empty. Consequently, other compulsive behaviours may sometimes co-exist – such as eating disorders, drinking, smoking, taking drugs, shopping or gambling.

You may find it difficult to build small treats into your day which would help you to get through it. For example, where someone else may enjoy anticipating their coffee break or a walk in the fresh air at lunchtime, you won't look forward to those things. You may even take pleasure in working through breaks and skipping meals, as though denying yourself proved something good about you. You will, however, spend all day anticipating the sexual experiences you will engage in later and probably feel resentful of work or family obligations which deny you immediate access to the experience.

Whether a compulsion has included contact with others or not, and whether the person is a man or a woman, discovery often leads partners of those with sexual compulsions to start snooping in their belongings, checking their email, phone and computer for evidence of what has been happening. Some compulsive sex users actually ask their partners to monitor their behaviour and internet to stop them. Though it is understandable that either or both of you may think this is a solution, it often just creates more distrust and places more stress on the relationship. It also doesn't allow the partner with the compulsion to develop any sense of responsibility for what is happening or any sense that they can take control themselves.

In the whirlwind of emotions experienced following discovery, it may be a good idea for a partner to seek help for themselves, to try to organise their thoughts and get some support. It may be that your compulsive partner will agree to counselling with you, but they may still be adjusting to the idea that what started as a solution has become a very serious problem. It may be difficult, but try to avoid judgement and blame, as support is more likely to help a compulsive partner to recognise they have a problem. A calm approach allows you the space to talk about what is happening and to discuss alternatives, and the serious risks of continuing. If you seem supportive, rather than angry – however justified this may be – the risks if the problem continues will be demonstrated much more clearly. Once it is accepted all round that a problem exists you can begin making plans to deal with it together or separately.

Relate counsellors will be able to offer support to partners. Relate psychosexual therapists are trained to assess the level of difficulty which you may be experiencing and either work with you themselves or refer you to an appropriate alternative resource. Your GP may also be able to help. A list of national resources is included at the end of the book (page 253).

AFFAIRS AND INFIDELITY

Internet sex and sexual compulsion can feel very much like infidelity, and opinion about what constitutes an affair has changed very much in the past decade or so. Sex with someone other than a primary partner in an agreed monogamous relationship can clearly be counted as an infidelity. However, there are other behaviours, such as secret texting or online friendships, which partners often see as infidelities, some of which lie in a very grey area. The talking point on identifying infidelity below may raise some issues worth thinking about even if this isn't something which has ever affected you. These days, more than ever, there are opportunities for contact with other people which can be hidden from partners and it may be worth discussing and negotiating what you both feel is acceptable within the relationship before one of you makes a mistake.

TALKING POINT: IDENTIFYING INFIDELITY

What behaviours would you say constitute infidelity from the list below?

➤ Having a friend of the gender and sexuality that interests you, even if you don't have sex

➤ Having a friend with whom you do occasionally have sex, though neither of you are interested in a more committed relationship

➤ Having a friend to whom you send regular emails or texts, or engage with on social media, several times a day

➤ Sending messages with explicit sexual content

➤ Having conversations with an old flame, even though a meeting is highly unlikely because, for instance, they now live abroad

➤ Having sexual conversations with a stranger

➤ Starting a relationship with an avatar in an online computer game

➤ Having phone or internet sex with a stranger

➤ Having coffee and a catch-up with an old flame

➤ Not telling your partner about having coffee and a catch-up with an old flame

➤ Sending your old flames cards at Christmas

➤ Occasional one-night stands

➤ A single one-night stand

➤ Having someone you love and see regularly but with whom you have no sexual relationship, though you would consider it if you weren't already attached

➤ Having an ongoing sexual and love affair

➤ Being in love with someone you no longer see

There are many couples who, for whatever reason, do accept that they or their partner may have occasional or regular sexual relationships with someone else; this is known as polyamory. The crucial point about polyamory is that it isn't a secret; everyone involved knows about the others; indeed, sometimes, there may be a group sexual relationship. As a result, other liaisons don't threaten the primary relationship and they don't usually create problems.

Some couples find that swinging, where they both have sex with someone other than their partner – but with the knowledge, agreement and even presence of the other – helps keep their relationship fresh and alive. Other couples would be horrified to think their partner had any friendships which weren't shared by both of them.

Once one partner feels betrayed, it doesn't really matter whether you agree about what is and isn't infidelity. Arbitrary judgements are spectacularly unhelpful in a relationship crisis when you may feel your whole world has become topsy-turvy and all your certainties have disappeared.

You may think you knew how you would behave if you found out your partner was seeing someone else, but that certainty often disappears too. For instance, you may have stated with certainty that you could be pragmatic and forgiving, but then you may actually find yourself feeling vindictive and crazy. Or if you were sure you would show your partner the door, you may be shocked to discover that you want them more than ever. There is no template for post-affair behaviour, so there is a temptation to grasp at whatever your belief was beforehand. This can lead to precipitate behaviour, with families split apart only to be reunited and split again or living through hell because a couple is so determined to make a go of a lost cause.

Sexting

'Sexting', or flirting by text, often with explicit content or images, has become a major problem that can seriously threaten relationships. Sometimes it is a symptom of a bigger problem with the relationship or it can just occur as a result of boredom or opportunity. Some partners find it particularly difficult to forgive the amount of time that is spent engaging with the texts or the secrecy that may be involved. The fact that nothing sexual has occurred may even make matters worse, particularly if it seems there is an emotional rather than physical attachment involved.

It can sometimes be difficult to recognise that what you're doing could be upsetting to a partner. Moreover, everyone doesn't have the same ideas about what should be acceptable behaviour in a relationship. Some partners caught sexting or having a relationship compare their behaviour with others in order to justify it. This may be no help at all unless there was a prior agreement that this behaviour was acceptable.

Betrayal

Whatever the reason for the other relationship(s), it almost always affects sex with your partner if they see it as a betrayal. Quite often, the period in the immediate aftermath of discovery is a relatively placid and close time when couples talk a great deal and rediscover their sexual relationship. Some say this is when they've had their best ever sex. However, this may be followed by a relatively stormy patch when partners want to know every detail of what happened and when. Sex then may feel out of the question.

Partners often don't believe what they are told, but demand more and more information, which becomes increasingly upsetting to them both. If you can possibly avoid this, it is much more helpful in the longer term to accept that knowing more won't alleviate the hurt and damage. Sometimes it is just a matter of waiting for a time when the pain subsides a little and it is possible to begin to rebuild trust and move forward.

Assuming you both want to make a go of the relationship, it can be hard to know how to behave. The 'betrayed' partner may not want to let the other off the hook too easily but also realises that nothing can change unless they are able to let the past go. Clearly, this is easier said than done. However, it is sometimes possible to agree to pretend that the relationship is okay for a while, just to try out what that feels like and whether it is possible. After all, at some point you do want the relationship to feel better, so it can help to experiment with that to see how it feels. You may also need a break from the recent pain and recriminations, which can be utterly exhausting.

Many couples say they want to go back to the way things were, but the way things were presumably provided the circumstances for the infidelity – so this is just what you don't want. In fact, the clunkier things feel, so much the better. This demonstrates that you are doing things differently and are in a phase of learning and development which will help prevent problems in future. It is a cliché but many couples emerge on the other side of an affair with a much better appreciation of themselves and their relationship, no longer taking either for granted.

There is a widespread belief that, whatever form it takes, an affair is the worst thing that can happen to a relationship. There is no doubt it *can* be devastating. However, it can be the more mundane and ordinary aspects of life which pose the greatest ongoing challenges, as the next chapter demonstrates.

Chapter Nine
Ageing

Big events and milestones tend to reverberate through our lives, affecting our relationships and sense of ourselves. Whether we think we have coped with resilience or suffered appallingly as each stage passes, there is likely to be some kind of adjustment to personal wellbeing or image at each stage. This can be positive, negative or a bit of both. For instance, leaving home or having a baby can both be seen as a gratifying sign of maturity – albeit sometimes accompanied by a shocking sense of grown-up responsibility.

Indeed, it is often a significant event, such as starting a family, which first creates awareness of time passing. Until then, ageing may have been thought of as something that happens in the future; obviously, though, it is happening all the time. Even if we didn't know how old we were, there are times in our lives that we might consider to be especially significant.

Most problems associated with sex as we age are related to medical conditions or dissatisfaction with our bodies. There is considerable evidence that a satisfying sex life when you are younger doesn't just disappear as you age. There is also a 'use it or lose it' aspect, which suggests that regular sex prevents sexual problems from occurring, though this may be because you notice them earlier if your sexual behaviour is frequent. Nevertheless, there are indications that regular intercourse in women may prevent or delay vaginal atrophy, a condition in which penetration can become difficult due to thinning of the vaginal walls and dryness. There may also be associated urinary problems, including a frequent need to wee and infection. In men, continued regular sex may make erectile dysfunction less likely to occur, with regular ejaculation thought to possibly reduce the risk of prostate cancer.

Older couples often report spending several hours making love, stopping and starting and making an occasion of it. Indeed, it is perfectly possible to have more time and energy for lovemaking once you have retired than you did in your youth. Unfortunately, outdated attitudes to older and disabled people having sex make some couples feel they shouldn't. Often, it is the couples themselves who judge what is okay. Couples who have lived together for a long time may end up thinking the same way and sharing the same unhelpful ideas. Because they don't challenge one another, they assume this is the only way to think and the way everyone thinks.

Yet there are many benefits to health and wellbeing in continuing sexual activity for as long as possible. Sex improves the supply of oxygen to the brain and may promote the growth of new brain cells, so being sexually active throughout your older age may help to keep dementia at bay. What's more, anti-ageing hormones are released after sex; sex also promotes skin renewal and prevents myriad diseases including osteoporosis. More on the health benefits of sex is explained on page 12.

AGEING IN MEN

Men and women are thought to reach their sexual peak at different ages – men in their late teens and women in their thirties. After this, some changes in sexual response begin to occur, though they may be extremely subtle and difficult to notice. Men may notice their hair thinning and some weight gain, sometimes involving the development of 'man boobs', and this can lead to lack of confidence and sexual avoidance in some men. Coupled with some loss of energy and family or work stress, it is easy to see how likely it can be to let your sexual relationship slip in middle age. However, this is far from inevitable and can be dealt with by watching your diet, taking exercise and making a conscious effort to maintain intimacy and make time for your relationship. Try not to assume that sexual decline is a natural consequence of ageing, as it certainly needn't be.

Erectile dysfunction

Any loss of erectile firmness may be seen as a problem, though often it is very minor. This may be why half of the men over 50 questioned in surveys *say* they have erectile problems. However, it is completely normal for men to need more stimulation to get and maintain an erection as time passes. By middle age, it is also normal for erections to come and go during lovemaking, especially when a man is paying attention to his partner, with no direct stimulation for himself.

Your partner may be upset by this, assuming you do not find them attractive. However, where just thinking about sex would produce a rock-hard erection in your teens, more targeted stimulation needs to be sustained to produce a hard erection when you are older. Indeed, erections are unlikely to ever be as hard as they were in your youth – but you don't actually need a very hard erection for vaginal penetration. A firmer penis is usually necessary for anal sex. However, a *very* soft erection is unlikely to be a problem unless penetration is attempted too soon.

It helps if partners are willing to offer more stimulation to keep the erection firm, but there is no reason to feel embarrassed about stimulating yourself. This may be more efficient and simpler, but may need to be explained to your partner beforehand if this is a new practice. It is probably worth getting into this habit before it is really necessary, so that any such changes have less impact as you get older.

Longer to climax

In addition, you may find that it takes longer to climax, that the ejaculation is less forceful and that the quantity of semen produced gradually diminishes. It may also become harder to recognise the *point of inevitability*, when ejaculation is imminent. After climaxing, the time until an erection is possible again (the *refractory period*) may lengthen. Sometimes it can be a day or two before penetration is possible again. This can make intercourse even more special and precious, especially if you have more time to indulge in lovemaking.

Enlarged prostate

An enlarged prostate affects more than half of men aged over 60 (see page 142). Because it presses on the urethra, the prostate can cause problems such as frequent trips to the loo at night, difficulty getting started when you wee and a poor stream, so that it may be hard to empty the bladder. Hygiene and confidence issues may make you avoid sex, but this is a condition which benefits from early advice and intervention. Often, little treatment is required other than changes to diet – for instance, avoiding anything which irritates or stimulates the bladder, such as caffeine, citrus and tomatoes – but there is no point in delaying medical advice and monitoring.

Low testosterone

Testosterone levels normally decline gradually in men but sometimes a more rapid drop occurs which results in symptoms including tiredness, loss of libido and erectile difficulties. If you are experiencing these symptoms, you should always consult your GP, as it is a simple matter to check your testosterone level and prescribe replacement therapy if it is low. Losing weight, and treating other underlying conditions, such as type 2 diabetes, can also help improve testosterone levels.

AGEING IN WOMEN

Women evolve into their sexuality and often find their interest in sex and responsiveness fluctuates at different times. Women are more obviously affected by hormone changes, both during their menstrual cycle and related to pregnancy and the menopause. These events may affect interest in sex but this is more due to the effects of pregnancy and menopause than as a direct effect of the hormones on libido. Other factors, such as tiredness, sexual boredom and even just an expectation that libido will diminish as we age, can be responsible for loss of desire. However, sexual experience and experimentation can considerably enhance sexual interest and responsiveness in women, many finding sex becomes more enjoyable as they age.

The menopause

Some women become much more sexually relaxed and adventurous after the menopause. This may be because you feel more confident about yourself and your relationship, less concerned with pregnancy and menstruation, and have more time and energy for sex. This can come as a delightful surprise or as a shock to partners if they were used to being the one pursuing sex. Some men even develop performance anxiety and erectile problems for the first time as a result. Expecting some changes to occur in personal style can help to prepare you for any differences.

The menopause is usually referred to as the period of about 10 years when women's ovaries start to produce less oestrogen and ovulation occurs in fewer cycles. Menstruation occurs less frequently and regularly. Finally, when no further eggs are available, menstruation ceases altogether. The menopause is then said to have occurred, though contraception should still be used for at least six months after the last period if you are over 50, to be sure periods have stopped completely. You should continue to use contraception for at least a year if you are younger. Bleeding or spotting long after periods have stopped requires medical attention.

The years before menopause, when symptoms are present, are known as the peri-menopause. It is during this time that women begin to experience erratic periods, tiredness, hot flushes, night sweats and mood swings. In some women, heavy periods can be so bad that they cause anaemia. Night sweats can also be so severe that you need to shower or change the bedclothes. Snuggling up with your partner may be difficult if it makes you hot, and partners can find this difficult to understand. If their nights are very disturbed, couples sometimes resort to separate beds or even bedrooms. Strategies are available to alleviate these symptoms, so it is worth discussing options with your GP. Hormone replacement therapy may help, as may keeping a diary to try to identify any foods or activities which provoke hot flushes.

The combination of symptoms can make it very difficult to feel sexual or even physically affectionate, if close physical contact brings on flushes. If you have the energy, rear entry or being on top are probably the least hot positions for intercourse, and oral sex can allow less heat-producing skin-to-skin contact. Making love in the shower may also provide a solution. It is worth making the effort to continue affectionate and sexual contact as it can be hard to reclaim this aspect of your life if you let it slide. If this happens, and you want to resume sexual contact, do make the effort to talk about it.

There is a view that because women can't have babies after the menopause they inevitably go off sex. However, it may be the effects of the menopause (such as the sweats and dry vagina) which put women off sex rather than clinical loss of libido. The hormone testosterone is more responsible for sexual interest than oestrogen, which is the hormone diminished by menopause. Though testosterone does decline very gradually throughout life in both men and women, testosterone levels are unlikely to be hugely affected until several years after the menopause. Sexual response in women often remains pretty healthy

– the clitoris may actually become more sensitive, for instance, and many women find their sexual interest improves.

Bear in mind that the clitoris has no role whatsoever in making babies, nor is the female orgasm remotely necessary for reproduction. Therefore, the idea that sex is redundant after the menopause is nonsense. Indeed, nature would prefer older couples to stick together to continue raising their children and grandchildren.

Having said this, menopausal symptoms don't necessarily stop when your periods do and the loss of oestrogen after the menopause does have some effects on sexual functioning. Uterine cramping or a dragging sensation associated with orgasm may be experienced, for instance. As already mentioned, continuing regular sex can help lessen issues such as loss of vaginal elasticity. Vaginal wetness may diminish significantly and be slower to occur, making intercourse painful. Oestrogen creams or pessaries can help, as can the use of lubricants. In both genders, arousal may take a little longer and orgasm may be less intense, though many older people say sex just keeps getting better.

As mentioned in Part One, a good couple relationship and sexual contentment help people to avoid, or not be so bothered by, physical symptoms – *and* to keep away depression and anxiety. Of course, there is a chicken-and-egg dilemma if physical symptoms prevent you from behaving sexually. But it should be clear by this point in the book that there is no limit to what is possible; there are always ways to feel sexual and behave sexually even if this requires some adaptation.

Many people feel much more relaxed about sex as they get older when worry about pregnancy has gone. For women, the absence of a menstrual cycle can make interest in sex more consistent and easier to manage. Both men and women often find that ageing is sexually liberating. They feel less tired, with no young children around, and they are generally freer to enjoy what they choose. It is other physical issues which may present some challenges to sexual expression and these will be discussed in the next chapter.

Chapter Ten
Physical Limitations

Despite *not* having been advised to give up sex, many people are nonetheless convinced that a physical setback is incompatible with lovemaking. A surprising number of those with a medical diagnosis are afraid to have sex or to ask for help, yet there are usually numerous ways to assist them to have sexual experiences safely and comfortably. Even people with significant spinal cord injuries and paralysis are able to be sexual, many enjoying orgasm and penetration. This isn't to say that physical challenges are always easily overcome. It often takes perseverance and creativity. However, the first step to making changes is to develop a positive attitude which allows you to see yourself as a sexual being and part of a sexual couple.

Some people feel that it is wrong to be sexual when they are ill and that they will be judged. Often, performance anxiety and embarrassment about having to ask partners to adjust simply prevents them from being sexual at all. However, for many conditions, experimentation and expanding one's sexual repertoire can offer numerous opportunities for sexual experiences.

Health professionals are sometimes reluctant to mention sex in case patients find the conversation intrusive or the timing is wrong, but this doesn't mean they aren't willing and able to help. Moreover, related charities and support organisations nearly all have information about sex on their website. Some also have helplines and specialist staff who have the knowledge and experience to advise you.

Your GP or practice nurse should also know of expert organisations in your area. Some of the national support groups are listed at the end of the book (see page 245). Do use them; the information in this chapter is only intended as a first step to encourage you to seek and obtain the professional medical support you need.

PELVIC INFLAMMATORY DISEASE (PID)

PID is caused by infection which has become widespread in the woman's reproductive organs. This can be caused by sexually transmitted conditions, such as chlamydia, but other infection can also be a cause. Because it can cause quite serious illness and infertility if left untreated, unexplained pelvic pain and pain during intercourse should always be investigated. Leaving an infection can cause adhesions to develop, whereby organs stick to one another, causing chronic pain. There is no reason, in any case, to put up with pain, especially as it can limit or prevent sex.

ENDOMETRIOSIS

Another cause of adhesions is endometriosis, a condition in which cells which form the lining of the womb (endometrium) appear in other areas throughout the pelvis. A common site is behind the womb, just beyond the cervix in an area known as the pouch of Douglas. This can cause particular pain on deep penetration, though intercourse may cause pain anyway. The cells in affected spots develop with the menstrual cycle and so may bleed into the pelvic area, leading to inflammation and infection. As the symptoms tend to diminish after a period, the condition can be difficult to diagnose. It is, therefore, important to persevere in seeking a diagnosis and treatment if any pelvic pain persists. Meanwhile, shallow intercourse, particularly in a side-to-side spoons position, may be the most comfortable, if intercourse is possible at all.

OVARIAN CYSTS

Though they often cause no symptoms, ovarian cysts can sometimes be a cause of pelvic pain. Most commonly, these fluid-filled sacs develop on the ovaries during the menstrual cycle and disappear of their own accord. Sometimes, though, they persist and continue to grow, pressing on the ovaries which causes pain and makes intercourse uncomfortable. Their size may also cause pressure on the bladder or bowels and make it difficult to open the bowels or make you want to wee a lot. Menstrual irregularities and bloating are also possible.

It is essential to always have symptoms checked as, rarely, ovarian cysts can contain cancerous cells. Large cysts may occasionally burst; to avoid this, it may be decided they should be surgically removed. If they are causing annoying symptoms, this may be a huge relief. Often, it is possible to use keyhole surgery and to preserve the ovary, so recovery is fairly quick and fertility need not be affected.

MITTELSCHMERZ

Abdominal or pelvic pain in the middle of the menstrual cycle, known as 'Mittelschmerz' (German for 'middle pain'), sometimes occurs around the time of ovulation. As always, explaining to your partner what is happening means you can plan how to manage this together – keep mild pain relief and hot-water bottles handy – and your partner will understand why you feel under the weather and may be averse to sex.

Painful ovulation can occur every month or be provoked, worsened or noticed when there have been hormone changes. For instance, it may initially be noticed in the first menstrual cycle after having a baby, following a miscarriage or during the menopause. It is quite likely the pain will have occurred before but you may have put it down to a tummy upset or not noticed it, as it can be mild and fleeting. Hormonal imbalance, ovarian cysts or bad luck can mean it is more intense and may be confused with appendicitis, inflammation of the fallopian tubes (salpingitis) or pelvic infection. It usually only lasts for a few uncomfortable hours, but can persist for a few days. Women taking the contraceptive pill don't ovulate and so don't experience this, so taking the pill can provide a solution if the discomfort is very troublesome.

FERTILITY

The ovaries contain millions of follicles, some of which ripen into eggs during each menstrual cycle. The eventual release of one or more eggs can cause some irritation or disturbance to the ovary and surrounding area, which causes the discomfort. Sometimes ovulation is also accompanied by light bleeding or spotting. In the absence of bleeding, you will probably notice that vaginal discharge is clear and stretchy, indicating this is a fertile time.

If you are unlucky enough to have fertility problems, the disappointment as each month goes by can, in itself, strain the relationship. Subsequent infertility treatment can put almost unbearable pressure on even the most loving couple. Sex can easily become a mechanical chore, dictated by ovulation and associated with temperature-taking and record-keeping. IVF is especially arduous and those outside the relationship – friends, family and work colleagues – may have no idea what you're both going through. Support may, therefore, be hard to come by and you may find it increasingly difficult to support each other. It may be no help at all to know that more than a quarter of pregnancies don't end with a live baby when everywhere you look there seem to be healthy babies and children.

Indeed, contraception and unwanted pregnancy can create years of practical and emotional challenges – then you find yourself immersed in trying to become pregnant and, if you're lucky, adjusting to having a baby. The more comfortable you are with physical and emotional intimacy before attempting pregnancy, the more readily you may be able to make it work for you subsequently. Regularly kissing and cuddling without sexual intent is a wonderful habit to ensure you continue physical connection and closeness even when sex isn't possible. Maintaining intimacy is important to your overall wellbeing as well as keeping the focus on you as a couple and not entirely on baby-making.

Similarly, thinking about holidays and breaks to look forward to *before* you begin the process of making babies or investigating infertility means you will make time for your relationship as well as for trying to become pregnant. Sufficient leisure and time off from any treatment or tests also helps relieve stress and promotes your health and wellbeing as individuals and as a couple, putting you in the best shape to conceive.

PREGNANCY

Once over the early nausea, you may find pregnancy is a very active time for you sexually, especially as some pregnant women find it easier to orgasm (though some also find it more difficult). As the bump grows, side-by-side intercourse is often more comfortable. Another comfy position may be lying at the end of the bed, knees up, supported by pillows if necessary, with your partner kneeling in front of you.

Nausea and fatigue put some women off sex in the early weeks of pregnancy. It is perfectly safe to continue intercourse throughout pregnancy unless you experience any heavy bleeding, once your waters have broken or as advised by your midwife or doctor. Until then, it can be a bonding and relaxing experience which cannot harm your baby. Indeed, once you reach full term, your midwife may suggest sexual arousal and orgasm as a way to induce or accelerate labour. Sex won't cause premature labour, however.

Sex after pregnancy

Sex once your baby arrives may seem like a scary prospect, especially if you have stitches. Your breasts may feel sore and be leaking milk, making it uncomfortable to hug your partner or even consider sex. Furthermore, arousal can encourage the breasts to leak, or they may start to feel hard and sore. Lots of cautious cuddles until any bleeding stops, your breasts feel more comfortable and any stitches heal will allow you to gradually consider lovemaking once again. Then very gentle, tentative sex may feel more possible.

If you are considering intercourse, make sure you are well lubricated and aroused before penetration is attempted. You may choose to use additional water-based lubrication for reassurance, but women often find intercourse after a baby is much more comfortable than they had feared. Any lingering pain from stitches or tears usually fades during the coming months; it is worth having any pain or discomfort medically checked though, if only for the assurance that all is as it should be.

MUSCULOSKELETAL DISORDERS

Unsurprisingly, joint pain significantly influences sexual behaviour in those affected by both rheumatoid and osteoarthritis. As well as physical difficulty, including limited mobility and stiffness, associated fatigue and depression appears to affect libido. Recent studies have shown that people with arthritic pain are among the least likely to seek or take up help to continue or resume sexual activity. This may happen because both partners have chronic conditions and their energy is taken up with coping. By the time you feel these are managed well, and you feel more like being sexual, you may think the moment has passed, but help should continue to be available, however old you are or however long your condition has continued.

Back pain

Understandably, chronic back pain can have an extremely negative effect on sexual relationships. This is not just due to the limitations imposed by pain but because partners are often frightened of causing more discomfort, which may occur powerfully and suddenly during intercourse. Also, partners may be willing participants but then suffer pain and stiffness for days afterwards. Experimentation and planning, taking analgesia before intercourse and resting afterwards can all help. Moreover, some people report that sexual activity actually improves their pain and overall sense of wellbeing.

Adequate back support and positioning for intercourse are significant in preventing post-coital pain. Frequent changes of position are helpful, as is the use of pillows or a foam wedge to improve back support. Some men like to sit in a chair, which supports their back well, with their partner straddling them during penetration. Arranging your bodies at right angles in an L shape can also relieve back pressure. Some men find standing for rear entry more comfortable than sitting or lying. Women may prefer a position where they can lean forward over pillows. Another possibility is lying side by side with the man behind the woman (spooning). Leaving thrusting to your partner may also be helpful.

FIBROMYALGIA AND CHRONIC FATIGUE SYNDROME

The above strategies may also be helpful for anyone experiencing pain and stiffness from fibromyalgia. Exhaustion alone is often a reason for avoiding sex, as fibromyalgia causes tiredness and can be a feature of chronic fatigue syndrome and other conditions. In addition, affected men may develop erectile dysfunction and women may experience vulval sensitivity and vaginal dryness, which can cause painful intercourse. Partners need to know that these conditions are real and not an excuse to avoid sex.

Many of those affected by chronic fatigue seem to have previously led very busy, active lives, and to have exacting standards, and so may find the limitations of the condition particularly distressing. If sex and closeness have been casualties of the condition, you could still gradually reintroduce cuddles and erotic touch. First agreeing with your partner that penetration and orgasm are a low priority should help to remove pressure and expectations which are disappointed. Treatment for erectile difficulties and vulval conditions is also important to improve your confidence and help you to feel supported. It can be a challenge to regard your body as capable of giving you pleasure as well as pain and distress, so patience and perseverance are required.

BREAST CONDITIONS

Mastitis, an inflammation of the breast tissue, is often associated with lactation but can affect women at other times too, causing high temperature, extreme pain and redness in the affected breast, making sexual touch out of the question. Though it is treatable with antibiotics, it is extremely unpleasant while it lasts and can restrict normal daily activities.

Breast surgery, whether it is cosmetic or to remove cysts or lumps, can be worrying and may affect sensation in your breasts. Surgeons generally aim to cause as little evidence of surgery as possible, so may make their incision around the nipple where a scar is less visible. This can cause some loss of sensitivity, which both you and your partner may find distressing, though sensation will probably return given time. Some lumpiness around the scar may also be present for a few months, though this usually disappears.

There is no reason to avoid touching the breast area once it has healed, though both of you may feel self-conscious about doing so. You may also avoid talking about this in case you make one another uncomfortable, so it can help to start the conversation *before* surgery when you may both be feeling less sensitive.

CANCER

A cancer diagnosis is clearly a devastating blow for any couple and sex may be the last thing on your mind. Nevertheless, couples who are supportive of each other and able to maintain some form of intimacy during treatment often report fewer relationship and general health problems subsequently.

A supportive partner is enormously important in easing issues with body image, which are so common following surgery. Any surgery affecting the reproductive organs, genitals or breasts clearly has the potential to affect sexuality and feelings about masculinity or femininity, as can hair loss. Though you may feel anything but sexy during treatment, and nausea can be a barrier to closeness, warm hugs and kisses may be appreciated by you both when you feel up to touch. Don't worry if that doesn't happen immediately; you need to feel comfortable and shouldn't put yourself under pressure.

You may not feel up to it before the treatment, but it can be helpful to have some sort of a plan to manage physical closeness following surgery, even if the plan changes. For instance, you might decide to initially wear a top in bed following breast surgery, both to protect the wound and allow you time to adjust. If this was the agreement, neither of you will feel so hurt if it is what one of you wants. If your partner is frightened of doing some harm, and so avoids sex and cuddles after surgery, you may need to initiate some physical closeness yourself. Otherwise, you could both carry on walking on eggshells indefinitely. A prior agreement that you will dictate the pace of physical intimacy may assist with this.

Sometimes, a cancer diagnosis actually brings couples closer. Indeed, three-quarters of respondents in some surveys say this is the case. However, about half admit to developing sexual issues. Avoidance of sex may simply be due to extreme fatigue, especially while having radiotherapy. Some sexual problems are also caused by chemotherapy, including off-putting nausea, thrush, vaginal irritation or dryness and mouth ulcers. Premature menopause following some treatments can be an issue for women, who may be treated with testosterone to restore libido. Hair loss, weight gain or loss and sore skin can add to self-consciousness and threaten feelings of attractiveness – but be reassured that they do pass. The earlier you seek advice about any remaining physical issues and help with sexual and relationship difficulties, the more likely they are to be successfully resolved. Many hospitals have specialist nurses who are used to tackling sexual issues, as do many charities, so it's worth speaking to them when you are ready. Expecting to experience some of these effects means you may be pleasantly surprised if they don't appear and not taken by surprise if they do. Taking opportunities to discuss your experience can be helpful; some hospitals have specialist groups where you can meet others in a similar situation and there are numerous online forums. Individuals and couples who have been through cancer already often have excellent advice and are proof that you are not alone in what you are going through.

CARDIOVASCULAR DISEASE

Having had a heart attack is no bar to sex. Following a heart attack, however, apparently three-quarters of us decrease or cease sexual activity, usually due to fear of another attack. Chest pain and breathlessness caused by any exercise should always be investigated, but advice is usually that gentle exercise, including sexual activity, can be gradually resumed. Indeed, daily exercise is encouraged after cardiac surgery and doctors often advise that intercourse is fine so long as you can walk up a couple of flights of stairs without undue breathlessness or any chest pain. Nevertheless, men should be aware that medication for the heart condition and accompanying vascular disease can both cause erectile difficulties. Sometimes, the first sign of cardiovascular disease can be erectile problems, so it is always worth seeking medical advice as soon as possible.

If you or your partner are fearful that sex could put too much strain on your heart, resume sexual activity slowly, starting with deep kissing and gradually increasing sexual touch and activity to orgasm. Monitoring breathlessness and pain will demonstrate what is possible and you should gradually be reassured that sex can remain a part of your life.

DIABETES

Erectile difficulties are sometimes associated with maturity onset diabetes, which can easily go unnoticed and untreated. Sensation and arousal may also be affected and you may have increasing difficulty in achieving orgasm. Diabetes can be responsible for recurring yeast infections like thrush, which can make sex difficult by causing soreness and itching in the mouth and genital area. Physical contact should be avoided until treatment is successfully completed.

PROSTATE CONDITIONS

The prostate is a small gland, about the size of a walnut, which lies below the bladder, surrounding the urethra, in men only. It secretes a whitish fluid, which contributes to most of the semen. This protects the sperm and enables them to move. Stimulation of the prostate via the rectum, either with the fingers, a vibrator or through anal intercourse, can result in orgasm.

A number of conditions can affect the prostate. It sometimes enlarges as men age and can cause pressure on the urethra as a result. It is also the site of one of the most common cancers in men.

Chronic pelvic pain syndrome

Chronic pelvic pain syndrome, which affects up to 16 per cent of men at some point in their lives, is responsible for almost all cases of prostatic inflammation. Though it is characterised by chronic pain in the genital and pelvic area, there may also be pain associated with passing urine and ejaculating. Often, no obvious cause is identified, as there is no infection present and no history of trauma. Unfortunately, there can also be erectile difficulties and problems with orgasm (discussed in more detail on pages 162 and 166). This frequently leads to loss of desire and/or avoidance of sex altogether. This is unsurprising given the pain, distress and stress caused by the condition, and the difficulties with diagnosis and treatment. Many men find the condition embarrassing and are reluctant to seek medical help or tell their partners what is happening. However, the sooner it is addressed, the less chance there is of sexual and psychological consequences and the greater the chance of finding ways to manage the symptoms.

Prostate cancer

Most of the symptoms of prostate cancer involve urinary abnormalities, but erectile problems may also be caused. Because symptoms are so similar to those caused by benign prostate conditions, it is always worth having any urinary or genital symptoms checked as soon as possible. A variety of different treatments are available for prostate cancer, depending on the type of tumour and its size. Some treatments are more radical than others and may cause sexual problems, but your surgeon will be able to explain the possible side effects and potential treatments in advance. Removal of the prostate is a common procedure to treat both cancer and a benign enlarged prostate which is causing unpleasant symptoms, such as frequent weeing during the night or a poor stream. Some operations remove the semen-producing organs with the prostate, which leads to dry ejaculation. A different operation may cause you to ejaculate backwards into the bladder, so that the semen is passed when you next wee.

If you are a man who enjoys anal stimulation or penetration, you may find that the sensations you experience will change without your prostate gland. Difficulties with erection, early ejaculation and orgasm may be temporary or lasting, but there are ways of managing the problems you may encounter, both medical and psychological. Though it can be several months before the extent of any problems is apparent, as they may improve alone, this is not a reason to avoid intimacy if you feel like being physically close or making love. Indeed, the more you behave sexually the more able you will be to determine what has changed and what problems are improving. Experimentation is important – don't be afraid you could cause damage once initial healing has occurred. Some of the exercises to retrain your erection and manage ejaculation and orgasm in the chapter on sexual dysfunctions (see pages 153–181) can be used to help you resume sexual activity. A positive, can-do attitude may be half the battle in finding ways to enjoy satisfying sexual experiences.

OVERACTIVE BLADDER AND INCONTINENCE

An enlarged prostate can put considerable pressure on the bladder, leading to frequent trips to the loo at night and dribbling. Cystitis, overactive bladder and numerous other bladder conditions can cause the urgent need to wee in both men and women, and stress incontinence can cause leakage in certain positions; for instance, when coughing, shouting or laughing. Many men and women avoid sex just because this causes so much embarrassment. With most of these conditions, going to the loo before sex doesn't stop you from wanting to go again a couple of minutes later, so you may be up and down during any sexual encounter. It may affect your confidence regarding hygiene and mean you avoid oral sex, and you may be too embarrassed to explain to your partner why. Some people won't even get close to their partner for a hug in case they smell of urine. Some bladder problems, such as painful bladder syndrome (PBS) or interstitial cystitis (where the bladder is continuously irritated and painful), can cause painful intercourse too.

Sadly, a huge number of people live with their fears and concerns without seeking help, though there is a huge amount that can now be done to treat the problems and/or help you to live with them, including being sexual. You must seek treatment if you are experiencing pain, passing blood or your urine smells unusual or fishy. Apart from anything else, it may be much easier to talk to your partner about the problems once you know what is going on and that something is being done about it.

As well as medical treatment, you may be able to train your bladder to go to the loo less often by weeing regularly every half hour or hour and gradually increasing the interval until you can wait for a couple of hours. Mindfulness exercises (see pages 43 and 91) have been used very effectively to deal with pain. Some food increases bladder irritability, particularly anything citrus or which includes caffeine, such as chocolate, tea, coffee and fizzy drinks. Alcohol and smoking may also be implicated.

Pelvic-floor exercises

Pelvic-floor (Kegel) exercises may also be helpful. These exercise the muscles you would use if you were to stop weeing in mid-flow, and you can locate them by doing this the first time only. (Don't attempt to stop weeing if you have any difficulty emptying your bladder.) Tightening and relaxing the muscles you used to stop the flow of wee can help to strengthen the pelvic floor. You can squeeze and hold for a few seconds and then release, and also do quick tighten and release exercises. Begin with 10 of each twice a day and gradually build up the number you can manage. You should feel the tightening in the genital and anal area, not the buttocks, tummy or legs. Women can place a finger into the vagina to feel the tightening and men will see their penis move if they do the exercises with an erection. Some people report enhanced sexual pleasure as well as improved bladder control when they perform these exercises regularly.

BOWEL PROBLEMS

There are many tummy and bowel issues which can make sex difficult or embarrassing, from constipation to managing a stoma (an opening on to the abdomen for passage of urine or faeces).

Irritable bowel syndrome

Irritable bowel syndrome (IBS) is a particularly common problem which often exists alongside other conditions, such as fibromyalgia or interstitial cystitis. It involves episodes of constipation or diarrhoea, or both, often accompanied by flatulence and bloating. It is thought that only about a quarter of those affected seek medical help, though IBS is treatable. It also needs to be differentiated from other bowel conditions which can do more damage if they are left alone – thus, self-medicating is not a good idea.

If pain or urgent diarrhoea is a problem, you may choose to avoid naked sex during flare-ups. However, you can still enjoy cuddles and try to make the most of the time in between episodes. Stress and diet may impact the condition, so it is worth keeping a diary to see what affects it. Sugar, fat, caffeine and alcohol are common culprits. Some of our clients have noted that fear of flatulence or diarrhoea happening during sex can bring them on. This means that special occasions and holidays, when sex might be expected, are ruined by performance anxiety unless a way to relax can be achieved. Practising mindfulness (see pages 43 and 91) and sharing your fears may help alleviate anxiety.

BRAIN INJURY AND STROKES

Brain injury, whether caused by a stroke or an accident, can turn your world upside down. However, regaining intimacy is part of the recovery process and it is thought that less than a quarter of those with an active sex life give it up following a brain injury. Nevertheless, it does present a number of challenges. Some people lose their sexual inhibitions, which may make for a great new sex life or be embarrassing if, for instance, they make inappropriate comments to a stranger. Some perceptual changes and differences in behaviour, personality and memory are also fairly common, so that it can seem as though you are making love to someone new, who is behaving in unfamiliar ways.

After a brain injury, you may experience some loss of sensation, taste or smell, which creates a different sexual experience and can affect your confidence, making patience and perseverance a necessity for both of you. Sexual problems do occur, including erectile problems, changes in sexual interest and difficulties with orgasm. These are sometimes due to the brain injury itself but often occur as a side effect of medication, so it is always worth getting them medically checked. Function may return given time or there may be help available, such as changing medication or referral to psychosexual therapy.

The biggest problem for couples may be a difference in the relationship itself if the affected partner requires a great deal of care. It can feel uncomfortable to make love with someone who is dependent and vulnerable, especially if they are also at all confused. Counselling can offer support and give you time to work out what you both want from your sexual relationship now and in the future.

OBESITY

Being overweight can make it difficult to find comfortable positions for intercourse which don't leave you out of breath or require too much stamina. The conventional missionary position, with the man on top, can be very uncomfortable. It is also helpful to adopt positions which make it easier to reach the genitals if there is a lot of padding around them. The following positions may be worth exploring:

- If the person being penetrated lies on their side, legs bent, and brings the knees up slightly towards the chest – but without adopting a full foetal position – the one penetrating can kneel to enter, resting their hands/arms on either side of the body. If necessary, use a pillow to raise the hips of the one being penetrated to make insertion easier and thrusting less strenuous.
- To keep tummies apart, the penetrator lies on their back and the person being penetrated sits astride them, facing towards the partner's feet. They can guide insertion and experiment with fast or slow movement on the penis. The penetrator has access to the partner's body and genitals for additional stimulation.
- Lying right at the edge of the bed, with the knees bent, the person being penetrated opens the legs as far as possible while the partner stands or kneels upright to penetrate.

HERPES

A diagnosis of herpes can occur at any time and usually comes as a most unpleasant shock. The herpes simplex virus can cause painful blisters, which rupture leaving sores in the mouth (cold sores) and genitals. They are very easy to pass on; consequently, it is important not to have sexual contact (oral, genital or anal sex) while the blisters are active. Sometimes, the virus can be active but asymptomatic, so it is always worth using a condom and avoiding direct contact with other unprotected anal and genital areas. Also steer clear of sharing towels, flannels and sex toys, especially if one of you has herpes and the other seems not to.

The condition can lie dormant for many years, so it does not necessarily mean that a partner has been unfaithful if one of you suddenly develops herpes. The first outbreak is normally the worst and episodes diminish in frequency after the first couple of years, so most affected couples do manage the condition. There isn't a cure but tingling often precedes the development of blisters. Starting antiviral medication at this stage may help to limit the outbreak.

BALANITIS

Balanitis is an inflammation of the head of the penis and foreskin, if there is one. The affected area can be very irritated, red, hot and sore. There may also be a smelly discharge. It may be difficult or impossible to retract the foreskin and erections will be painful. Balanitis can be due to an infection, skin condition or allergy. For instance, you may develop an allergy to soap, shower gel or washing powder. Sometimes, spermicides, rubber contraceptives or lube can provoke an allergic reaction.

Often, balanitis occurs as a result of poor hygiene when there is a build-up of a thick, creamy material comprised of dead skin and secretions (smegma) under the foreskin. This can be avoided by daily washing with the foreskin retracted and ensuring the head of the penis is properly dried after urinating, washing or ejaculating (maintaining hygiene is also discussed on page 200).

Balanitis is usually easily treatable with antibiotics. However, it can keep recurring if the foreskin is especially tight and difficult to retract. This will also cause painful intercourse and, sometimes, painful masturbation. In such cases, it may be necessary to stretch the foreskin under anaesthetic or consider circumcision. This is a very common problem, so it is worth mentioning balanitis or tight foreskin to your GP as soon as you notice it. It is also important that your partner understands why you may be avoiding sex. There is no excuse for poor hygiene – which is off-putting for partners anyway – but partners can help with identifying possible allergens and may be keen to begin and/or end sexual encounters with a warm bath or shower together to help maintain cleanliness.

QUEEFING

A particularly embarrassing side effect of intercourse for many women is what's known as a 'vart', 'queef' or 'fanny fart'. During intercourse or exercise, air is pushed into the vagina and is then released, making a noise like flatulence. This isn't flatulence, however, and there is no smell or associated rumbling tummy. It is especially common when changing sexual position or as the penis is withdrawn. Sometimes it just happens in the middle of sex.

Many couples find it disconcerting or hilarious, but some women avoid sex because they find it so embarrassing. However, it pretty much affects all women at some point, especially during vigorous or athletic sex; for some, it happens every time. If you feel embarrassed enough to avoid sex because of this, it is worth discussing with your partner in a non-sexual situation and planning how you would like it to be handled when it happens. Showing your partner this section of the book will get the conversation started if you can't find the words. Rest assured that it is perfectly normal, very common, won't harm anyone and is completely outside of your control.

PELVIC ORGAN PROLAPSE

Some women can experience muscle laxity, especially following child-birth, which causes the bowel or bladder to put pressure on the walls of the vagina. The uterus may also protrude so low that the cervix can be seen at the vaginal opening, sometimes causing discomfort. Though this may affect your sexual confidence considerably, once arousal begins the vagina changes in readiness for penetration and the cervix recedes, so intercourse should still be possible. Focusing attention on the breasts and kissing until arousal is established may help you to relax. In some cases, there is accompanying incontinence or pressure from the bowel during intercourse makes it uncomfortable. Avoiding constipation and keeping up pelvic-floor exercises can help somewhat.

HYSTERECTOMY

Hysterectomy is the usual surgical treatment for prolapse, though a few surgeons offer an operation which involves supporting the pelvic organs and repairing the pelvic floor. This may be preferred if you want to have more children and/or enjoy the feeling of uterine contractions during orgasm or deep penetration which stimulates the cervix. Some women miss this following hysterectomy. For the majority, though, it seems hysterectomy brings a great deal of relief by removing unpleasant symptoms such as a prolapse or heavy bleeding. Intercourse can be resumed after six to eight weeks when healing is complete. Orgasm may feel different, as may the sensations associated with intercourse as the vagina can be a little shorter.

If there has been complete removal of the ovaries, this will lead to an immediate menopause, which will need to be treated with hormone replacement therapy, usually applied via skin patches. Oestrogen creams or pessaries are prescribed to treat vaginal dryness; testosterone may also be prescribed – usually via a patch or gel – to help avoid difficulties with libido, osteoporosis and cardiovascular disease. Despite these effects, hysterectomy can produce a new enthusiasm for sex by restoring confidence and removing debilitating symptoms.

This section has offered ways to manage some of the limitations caused by physical conditions, but there are clearly many more which haven't been covered. The important message, though, is that there is usually some sort of solution to the difficulties you are experiencing. It is almost always easier to manage a problem if you are prepared to experiment and seek help as early as possible.

Don't keep your partner in the dark either. Though you may feel the problem is all yours, your partner probably wouldn't agree as it affects them just as much in terms of the possible intimacy between you. When sex and intimacy happens less often, partners so often imagine you have gone off them rather than that you are avoiding sex due to embarrassment or discomfort. When sexual dysfunctions do develop, you should both be involved in their treatment, as the next chapter explains.

Chapter Eleven
Sexual Dysfunctions

Some sexual problems are not necessarily related to other physical limitations but do manifest physically, presenting challenges to your sexual relationship. These are known as sexual dysfunctions because they are expressly related to sexual behaviour. However, they are often very manageable and are the kind of problem specifically dealt with by psychosexual therapists. These are a kind of relationship counsellor specialising in sexual issues. Their work is explained in more detail in Chapter Twelve (see pages 182–190).

Whether they have physical or psychological causes, or a combination of both, sexual dysfunctions can happen to anyone and are probably not related to the quality of your relationship or your sexual potential as a couple. They can occur at the beginning of a relationship or pop up unexpectedly after years with no problems at all. They can happen with all your partners or only one. Though those affected often assume the issue has only ever happened to them, or that there is no hope for dealing with it, read on and you will see how common and well recognised they can be.

PAIN AND DISCOMFORT

Pelvic pain and penetration problems can be present throughout someone's life, may develop over time or can come on suddenly. There are a number of reasons why they can occur, both physical and psychological (for more on pelvic pain see pages 133 and 143). Often, a physical cause understandably leads to a psychological response, which can produce a debilitating and chronic condition. This is one of the reasons why it is so important to have all unusual symptoms medically checked as early as possible, so that more complicated and difficult problems can be avoided.

Dyspareunia

Dyspareunia is the clinical term to describe painful intercourse in both men and women and is thought to be considerably more common than statistics suggest. Some women experience pain associated with ovulation at mid-month (see page 134) and even a small amount of spotting or bleeding can make deep penetration more uncomfortable. Post-menopausal pain during intercourse is discussed in the chapter on ageing (page 131) and is common due to lack of natural lubrication. Unsurprisingly, pain leads to tension and the avoidance of intercourse in both sexes.

Vaginismus

Women frequently, and involuntarily, tense their vaginal muscles in anticipation of pain, a condition which is sometimes referred to as vaginismus. It is now recognised that vaginismus is highly likely to develop as a response to dyspareunia and that vaginal tension will cause dyspareunia – therefore, the two conditions are seen as inextricably linked. But why do they occur? Some women are just plain terrified by the idea of inserting anything into the vagina, often having heard horror stories from thoughtless relatives or frightening playground rumours from friends when they were younger. For other women and girls, a problem can begin with something as simple as a clumsy attempt at tampon insertion, difficulties caused by a particularly tough hymen or other rare congenital abnormalities where the vagina has not developed in the usual way. For some women, issues start after childbirth. There can be difficulty in diagnosis and treatment, especially as pain can be real or imagined/anticipated, and an injury or cause does not always become evident.

Provoked vestibulodynia (PVD) and generalised vulvodynia

Some other conditions affect sensation in the female genital area. Provoked vestibulodynia involves vulvar discomfort, or even pain, which can feel like burning or stinging. The area near to the vaginal entrance, urethra and labia minora, the inner lips of the vagina, may become sore in response to any form of touch. This is unlike generalised vulvodynia, in which pain is not brought on by touching but just seems to occur of its own accord. It is not really understood what causes this, but it could be a combination of a number of factors. The variety of hormonal changes, injuries – especially in childbirth – and infections that can occur make it unsurprising that a chronic response can develop, where the pain and discomfort is always troubling. Some women may also have congenital abnormalities or other problems which make the condition more likely. For instance, it is thought that pain receptors are particularly sensitive in those affected. Unfortunately, therefore, other painful conditions may coexist, including interstitial cystitis, a painful inflammatory condition of the bladder. Fibromyalgia – which causes fatigue, pain and stiffness all over the body – is also common, as is irritable bowel syndrome.

As with painful intercourse, the potential variety of causes makes PVD difficult to diagnose. Medical practitioners are likely to look first at simple causes, such as injury in childbirth, rather than to seek out multiple reasons for the symptoms. Consequently, many women suffer for years before getting a diagnosis, which can delay effective treatment significantly. Touching the affected area causes considerable tenderness and can make it difficult or impossible to insert tampons or enjoy intercourse. Indeed, the condition is often diagnosed by touching the affected area gently with a cotton bud, as this alone can provoke PVD. Fear of pain can cause women to tense the powerful vaginal muscles, making it even more painful and difficult to touch the vulval area at all, let alone attempt sexual touching or intercourse.

You may be one of the 20 per cent of those affected who experienced symptoms while still in your teens or even younger (primary PVD/vulvodynia). Or you may be among the majority for whom symptoms begin later (secondary PVD/vulvodynia). However long this has gone on, you may sometimes think you must be imagining the pain. This is sometimes suggested by friends, partners or even doctors, who cannot imagine the problem could just develop out of the blue. But the pain is very real and becomes more debilitating as time wears on. This is exhausting, making you less tolerant and increasingly frustrated as well as, sometimes, really angry. Your partner may assume you have gone off them or that you are exaggerating, especially if repeated medical consultations have not helped.

Effect on relationships

Whatever the reason for genital/pelvic pain and penetration difficulties, they can have serious consequences for affected individuals and couples, made worse the longer you wait for help. However, these conditions are increasingly being recognised earlier and you should not give up trying to find a diagnosis and appropriate treatment.

Living with the difficulty is bad enough in itself, but it can lead to the development of a very negative self-image and relationship problems. It isn't just that some partners can be insensitive; your *expectation* that your partner may have a problem with your condition can be an issue in itself. You may fear that, however understanding they are, your partner will get fed up and find someone else. You may even think you have a duty to be sexual, whatever the personal cost, and feel you have failed. Though this may seem silly on a good day, on a bad one it is easy to become worn down with the discomfort and feeling that you will never be a normally functioning woman. It can be very isolating if others are unable to understand how so many aspects of your life are being affected. At the extremes, some women react by completely shutting down and avoiding sex and any form of touching or intimacy, while others endure painful sex.

Creative solutions

All genital pain conditions can lead to feelings of failure, isolation, difference and loss. Significantly, many women who have tense pelvic muscles can enjoy great sex without intercourse, and couples can be very creative sexually. Often, they only seek help if they want to start a family.

PVD, on the other hand, makes any form of genital touching very difficult, so erotic sexual touching may be limited to breasts and buttocks. Experimenting with other body touching to discover sensitive, erogenous areas can help. Many couples enjoy frottage, where the genitals are rubbed against an area of the partner's body to produce orgasm. When clothed, this is often called 'dry humping' (see also page 234). Movement of the mons, the padded area above the pubic bone, can sometimes stimulate the clitoris sufficiently to produce orgasm without touching or damaging the sensitive vulval area.

In the past, some gay women have reported reluctance to seek help in case there was an assumption that they wouldn't be interested in penetration – whereas vaginal exploration, insertion and penetration may or may not be a valued part of their sexual repertoire. However, thoughtless assumptions about people's sexual behaviour are diminishing, so psychosexual therapists and medical practitioners are much more interested now in individual needs and interests, rather than having fixed and stereotypical ideas.

CASE EXAMPLE: KATE AND FRANK

Though she had enjoyed sex in the past, Kate began to experience pain on intercourse shortly after her 45th birthday. She tried to hide this from her partner, Frank, but it was obvious he knew she wasn't enjoying sex any more. He tried to hurry 'so as not to bother her'. As a result, there was little foreplay and Kate hardly felt aroused at all when Frank entered her. This made sex even more painful and she became so tense that eventually sex became impossible. After the couple's last disastrous attempt, Frank got up and left the bedroom, feeling ashamed and upset that lovemaking had made Kate cry. He went to sit downstairs for a while to think, hoping Kate would have fallen asleep by the time he went back up.

Frank wondered if this was something to do with Kate's age. Or maybe she no longer found him attractive. He hadn't known how to bring the subject up, so it hadn't been talked about and now he was scared of what he might hear if they did discuss what he felt had become a major problem. He decided he would just have to resign himself to life without sexual intercourse.

Kate, meanwhile, was utterly devastated. She thought Frank had gone downstairs because he was angry and she felt ashamed that she wasn't being a 'proper wife' to him. She didn't know who to talk to or what to do. She didn't want to go to the GP in case she thought Kate was getting too old to be thinking about sex and would judge her. The whole thing was horrendously embarrassing to her. She was still awake when Frank came back. Though he turned his back on her, she put a hand on his shoulder and whispered that she was sorry. Frank turned towards her and patted her thigh: 'Don't worry,' he said. 'I won't bother you again.'

Frank thought he had let Kate off the hook. He assumed she would be relieved that he wasn't going to 'pester' her for sex any more. He avoided touching her in case she thought he was initiating intercourse and they became awkward around each other. They didn't seem to enjoy conversational banter the way they had; both were guarded and seemed low to their children, who kept asking what was up. They both became irritable about this and when Kate told them to pipe down and stop asking, Frank was convinced he had done the right thing in leaving her alone.

But Kate was heartbroken. She was very low and really missed the cuddles she and Frank had previously enjoyed. Now he barely looked at her. She wondered whether she should ask the GP for hormone replacement therapy even though she had no menopausal symptoms. Finally, she was invited for a routine smear test. Taking smears had never been a problem in the past, but this time she was so tense that the nurse couldn't take the smear. She also said she thought Kate's vulva looked a bit sore and asked the doctor to see her.

It emerged that Kate had a low-level fungal infection. This reminded her that she had had thrush a couple of years previously when she had been taking antibiotics for a throat infection. She started to wonder if this had anything to do with her pain. The doctor prescribed oral anti-fungal tablets for Kate and for Frank, just to be on the safe side. But this didn't improve their relationship. Frank seemed to think she was blaming him for her infection and the couple were barely talking. She had been asked to make a further appointment for her smear test, but this time she explained what had been going on and it was the nurse who suggested she think about psychosexual therapy.

Kate went to her first appointment without Frank and found it easier than she had expected to talk to the therapist. She was surprised that the therapist asked her questions about things she had taken for granted, like the idea she shared with Frank that sex diminishes with age. At one point, Kate mentioned how ridiculous she felt next to her daughter, who was in the sixth form at school and blossoming into a very beautiful young woman. She felt embarrassed to be in the room with her as it made her feel so dowdy; in the back of her mind she had been thinking that her own sexual life was nearing an end.

Saying this out loud was a turning point for Kate, especially as the therapist didn't think this was an unusual thought or blame her. The therapist did, however, say there was no reason why Kate and Frank couldn't go on enjoying intercourse and/or other sexual encounters for many years to come. That night Kate plucked up the courage to talk to Frank about what had been happening. He was astonished and relieved that Kate had cared enough to see someone to try to sort things out. Kate surprised herself by telling Frank that it was not all her problem. It could have been tackled earlier if they had both summoned the courage to talk to one another about it.

After a long discussion that night, the couple decided to try psychosexual therapy. They were given exercises to work on separately and together which helped them to reconnect sexually and, eventually, to enjoy their sexual relationship again, including intercourse.

Genital pain in men

Men also sometimes experience dyspareunia or pain on intercourse. About 20 per cent of men may have experienced some sort of pelvic pain in the past year and about 5 per cent of men may have pain during intercourse or ejaculation. Sometimes, this is caused by a tight foreskin, which can be treated (see also the section on balanitis, page 149). Some medical conditions, such as inflammation of the prostate gland, are responsible so you should always have pain medically checked. Chronic pelvic pain syndrome (CPPS) is discussed in more detail on page 143.

Persistent genital arousal disorder

Persistent genital arousal disorder (PGAD) is often triggered by sexual activity. Typically, following an orgasm, slight movement provokes another orgasm, which is followed indefinitely by more orgasms. Sometimes the orgasms can be triggered by less obvious stimuli, such as crossing the legs or going to the toilet. As the orgasms can last for up to several hours – or days in really extreme cases – the condition can be extremely debilitating. It affects both men and women, though it is more common in women, especially after the menopause.

More commonly, without any feelings of desire or erotic thoughts, women become aware of a congested feeling in the genital area, similar to that experienced during sexual arousal. Masturbation may be attempted to control it, but the feeling persists. This congested feeling may appear in addition to bouts of continuous orgasming or on its own. It can continue for days, weeks or months, disappearing as suddenly as it started and then resuming at some point in the future for no evident reason. Because sex can be a trigger, some people end up avoiding it altogether. There are reports that it has also sometimes been provoked by ceasing or changing SSRI anti-depressant medication. Nevertheless, PGAD can begin with no apparent provocation at all.

It isn't known how many people are affected but it may be a relatively common condition, as only really severe cases seem to be reported; many more people may be managing the condition by themselves.

Pelvic massage, distraction, identification of possible triggers, anaesthetics and nerve-blocking medication have all been used to treat PGAD, but it seems rather a hit-and-miss business. If you are unfortunate enough to be affected, do seek help as the more people come forward the more likely it is that the condition can be understood and solutions can be found.

ERECTILE DIFFICULTIES

One-off or occasional problems with erections are common, often associated with alcohol use. However, erectile dysfunction (ED), as it is known, is sometimes a consequence of cardiovascular disease, diabetes, neurological damage and a side effect of some drugs, including antidepressants. Consequently, it is essential to have ED checked if it persists. ED is less likely to have a clinical cause if you still have erections when you masturbate or if they still occur at other times, such as when you wake up in the morning. A large number of men *think* they have ED because their erections are less hard or frequent than they used to be, but it is entirely normal for this to start happening once you are out of your teens or twenties and so is not considered dysfunctional.

The good news is that there are several ways to treat ED and, in any case, very little firmness is needed for penetration. Moreover, many men are still aroused to orgasm, even with little or no erection. Nevertheless, it is not surprising if you find your ED distressing. Some men think of their erection as a friend and feel less of a man when they can no longer acquire their firmness on demand. If there is no clinical cause for your ED, a common reason is performance anxiety. Fear of losing an erection can make it disappear or stop it in the first place.

Nearly all men experience episodes of ED, especially when they are tired, stressed or run down. More chronic ED is often provoked following what would have been a one-off episode of ED caused by too much alcohol or anxiety. Fear of it happening again then *causes* it to happen; the more it happens, the more worry causes it to happen again.

Treatment of ED

Because it is so common, affecting about a third of men, numerous ways of treating it have been developed, both chemical and mechanical. Injections can be given directly into the base of the penis, or pessaries can be inserted into the urethra to cause a temporary erection. You can also achieve an erection using a vacuum device. When air is pumped into a cylinder placed over the penis, the blood vessels fill up, causing an erection. This is maintained with a band placed around the base of the penis. This is a good solution if you need a firmer erection for anal penetration when other methods have failed.

Hormones are sometimes prescribed where an imbalance is detected or you may be offered one of the oral PDE5 inhibitors, such as Viagra, Cialis or Levitra. These work in a similar way by blocking an enzyme which then facilitates erection with arousal. Levitra (vardenafil) may work most quickly of the three drugs, but it may be a matter of experimenting to see how long it takes for you. It is necessary to anticipate sex and take the medication as its potential effect wears off within a few hours. You won't get an erection unless there is arousal and this should go away following orgasm. Cialis (tadalafil) is sometimes prescribed in small daily doses for those who find pre-planning inhibiting or difficult. This means the effect lasts longer and you won't need to remember to take a tablet before having sex. Not everyone qualifies for NHS prescriptions for these pills, however. Recently, though, the generic versions of Viagra (sildenafil citrate) have been more widely prescribed on the NHS.

Unfortunately, because some men are so embarrassed about the condition, they try to find treatments on the internet rather than consulting their GP to assess their suitability for the drugs. As well as meaning you bypass important medical checks to ascertain the cause of the ED and ensure the drugs are suitable for you, you may not know what you are purchasing, what's in it or how to use it properly. You should *always* see your GP.

These drugs have some side effects and risks which need to be explained properly before you use them and you need to make sure that they are safe to take with any other drugs you are taking or with any medical conditions. The most common side effects include headaches, facial flushing, dizziness, blocked nose and tummy upsets. Cialis can sometimes also cause back pain. If you experience any serious unusual health problems after taking the drug – such as chest pain, racing pulse, faintness or erection lasting more than four hours – you must seek medical help urgently. These drugs aren't suitable if you have had a heart attack or stroke within the past couple of months or if you have some cardiovascular conditions, kidney or liver disease.

Some medications, especially nitrates and anticoagulants, are dangerous when taken in combination with PDE5 inhibitors. They don't work for everyone either. For instance, the bodies of people with retinitis pigmentosa lack the chemical which the drugs affect.

Moreover, it is advisable for all men to have testosterone levels checked before starting treatment as the drugs may not work as well, or at all, when testosterone levels are low.

If anxiety is responsible for your ED, it is possible to retrain yourself to regain your erection once it starts to disappear. Of course, this is less likely to work if there is a medical reason for the ED; however, anxiety often combines with a clinical cause to make ED worse. Many men use retraining exercises, such as the one below, *and* PDE5 inhibitors until their confidence returns, because an erection is needed for the exercises.

EXERCISE: WAX AND WANE

To complete this exercise:

➤ Stimulate the penis until it is erect and then allow the erection to go down without climaxing.

➤ Wait briefly, then stimulate to erection twice more before allowing yourself to ejaculate.

➤ This doesn't solve the problem of getting an erection in the first place, but it does help build confidence that you can get it back when it disappears. Just knowing this stops it from disappearing in some men.

When you feel skilled with the exercise, make it more difficult by stimulating in different ways, using different pressure or speed. If this goes well, and you can control your erection during masturbation, you can transfer the exercise to lovemaking and even ask your partner to help. The same sort of process should be followed, stimulating the penis to erection with hands or mouth and allowing it to subside twice before ejaculating with the third erection. This is likely to be more difficult than it was when masturbating. You will need to signal to your partner to stop if you feel you may climax. However, once mastered, this technique allows you to regain your erection whenever you want to. Many men simply reach down and touch themselves to bring their erection back. If you want to, you can even practise stopping and starting during penetration, allowing your erection to subside while inside your partner.

Remember, it is possible to be aroused to orgasm without an erection and you don't need an erection to stimulate your partner. You can use hands, mouth, sex toy or penis for partner arousal. Straight couples often enjoy rubbing the penis all over the vulval area; stimulating the clitoris can be highly effective even with a soft penis. Very little firmness is required to achieve vaginal penetration and sometimes the penis becomes harder inside the vagina if you feel relaxed enough. For anal sex, a semi-firm penis may sometimes be able to penetrate, though your partner would need to be well relaxed and prepared, and you would need plenty of lube.

AROUSAL AND ORGASM

Sex researchers Masters and Johnson used studies involving human subjects to identify what happens to the body during sex. They noted a sequence beginning with arousal which then reached a high level and plateaued. Though you will be aware of mounting arousal, you are unlikely to be aware of having reached the plateau phase; this relates more to the point close to orgasm where changes in the body cease. For instance, the pulse and breathing become faster with arousal but reach a point where they stop increasing. Similarly, the genital area fills with blood and, when no more can enter, the erection is as firm as it can be. Vaginal lubrication – which is there to prepare the vagina for penetration – reaches its maximum and also ceases.

Awareness of arousal may ebb and flow until just before orgasm. At this point, both men and women experience a series of rapid rhythmic contractions of the genitals and anus and of internal organs, such as the prostate in men and womb in women. Men ejaculate and immediately enter the resolution phase, where their body returns to normal. Women, meanwhile, are able to experience further orgasms before entering the resolution phase.

Early ejaculation

A huge number of men and their partners wish they didn't ejaculate so soon. Often, they have very unrealistic ideas about how long they should be able to keep thrusting during intercourse, often due to the way sex is portrayed. Many of the studies into how long thrusting continues have relied on self-reports and it is possible that respondents may have exaggerated their staying power. About 10 minutes is the most men have usually reported, though the majority will have climaxed by five minutes or so. For many couples, continuous intercourse probably often only lasts for two or three minutes before ejaculation. Early, premature or rapid ejaculation are the names used to describe very quick ejaculation, occurring before or as soon as penetration begins or after only a couple of thrusts.

For couples enjoying a range of sexual activities, even chronic early ejaculation – which is thought to affect up to a third of men – may not be a problem at all. However, even when your orgasm occurs within the average or expected time, you may wish you could last a little longer. It is not so much quick ejaculation that spoils sex but the time spent worrying about it. Extreme anxiety and focus on trying not to climax affects the overall quality of the sexual experience for you and your partner. It can be embarrassing and difficult to talk about, so some couples just avoid all sex. If you do attempt intercourse, it then becomes much more of a big occasion, increasing the likelihood of anxiety and early ejaculation. Inevitably, the less you have intercourse, the less comfort your body will have with the experience so that sex is always associated with anxiety and failure. Avoidance never gives you the opportunity to overcome that.

Early ejaculation often happens to younger men who have not yet learnt ejaculatory control. This is generally mastered relatively quickly, however, and does not develop into a chronic problem. Sadly, age and experience don't always help. It may be that some individuals have a genetic predisposition to early ejaculation and/or are particularly sensitive to hormonal and nervous-system responses when they are aroused. Nevertheless, worrying about it and focusing on not climaxing actually make it more likely to happen. Sometimes a single incident when you were anxious, perhaps with a special new partner, recurs simply due to fear of it happening again.

It has also been found that men with early ejaculation do not find their arousal or orgasm as satisfying as men who don't ejaculate early, possibly because they worry about it during sex or are rushing sex. Early ejaculation can be a result of hurrying orgasm during adolescence, usually for fear of discovery during masturbation, and this becomes habitual. Many men with early ejaculation also do not appear to recognise the 'point of inevitability', when an orgasm is imminent. This is because they have learnt to speed through arousal without focusing on the build-up and different enjoyable sensations it can produce. In learning to be sexual, orgasm has become the focus and goal, and the quicker the better.

Managing early ejaculation

Fortunately, improved ejaculatory control is relatively easy to learn. To retrain your responses, it is often helpful to practise what is known as a stop:start technique. Using this method, you masturbate to a high state of arousal, close to the point of inevitability, and then stop. After waiting a short while, possibly allowing your erection to diminish a little, masturbation begins again – once again stopping just before the point of inevitability. This process can be repeated three or four times before allowing yourself to climax.

This is a very simple process, but takes some mastering. Most men find it difficult to recognise the point of inevitability at first and have accidents, when they ejaculate unexpectedly. You probably need to change the way you masturbate from a quick, reflexive method, which you know will produce results, to a much slower, more languorous method. Handling your penis more gently, and really tuning in to the feelings this produces, will eventually help you to recognise the point of inevitability and develop more control. To begin with, this slower approach can be so pleasurable that you ejaculate even sooner, but eventually you will start noticing the point of no return and be able to stop before you reach it.

Once you feel confident that you have mastered the technique, you can start to try it out with your partner. Agree a signal which tells your partner to stop stimulating you and proceed as you did while masturbating. Again, a slower, more sensual approach may make it easier to recognise the point of inevitability and give the stop signal well in time. Experiment with manual and oral stimulation and expect to have some accidents. Eventually, you should be ready to try the stop:start technique during intercourse.

Stop:start and vaginal intercourse

If you habitually orgasm as soon as your penis is near the vulval area, use the stop:start process while touching the vulva with your penis. As your control improves, you or your partner can stimulate the vulva and clitoral area with your penis and become used to the sensations this produces. Finally, place the penis at the vaginal entrance – but don't penetrate until you are sure you recognise the point of inevitability in this position.

It then often works well to begin penetration by just allowing the penis to rest in the vagina after insertion, without any thrusting or movement of your partner's pelvic floor at all. Once your penis is used to being inside the vagina, movement can begin, with the same signal for your partner to stop when you are close to the point of inevitability. Allowing your partner to control penetration from above may also be a good way to get started. As your control improves, you should both have a great sense of achievement.

Stop:start and anal sex
A similar process works for anal sex but needs to incorporate condom use, plenty of lube and preparation for the receiving anus. Resting the penis inside the anus after initial penetration is always a good idea, to give it time to relax and accommodate the penis before thrusting begins (for more information about anal sex, see page 233).

These stop:start techniques require you to be relaxed and unhurried so should not be attempted when you are busy or stressed. Rather than planning the process themselves, many couples find it useful to seek the guidance of a psychosexual therapist – though rest assured that all exercises are done in private, not in the therapist's presence.

Savouring the experience

Mindfulness exercises, such as those on pages 43 and 91, are very helpful in developing an ability to focus on the here and now and really savour the experience of the moment. This can help tremendously to develop your awareness of arousal and your enjoyment, and lead to the all-important identification of your point of inevitability. This is vital as it is thought that many early ejaculators may even climax before they have reached full arousal. It may also help to deal with intrusive thoughts, including worry about climaxing early.

The pharmacology industry is still struggling to find a drug which cures early ejaculation effectively. This may be because there are so many possible causes. However, some antidepressants (SSRIs) do slow down ejaculation and have been used to treat early ejaculation very effectively.

Difficulty climaxing in men

Unfortunately, for some men, rapid ejaculation would be welcome, as they have great difficulty in climaxing. The technical terms which may be applied to difficulty associated with climaxing include inhibited, retarded or delayed ejaculation and male orgasmic disorder. This usually refers to problems attaining orgasm during intercourse or with a partner, as the issue may not be associated with masturbation. It can happen occasionally to anyone and would rarely be seen as a difficulty unless either or both partners were concerned by it and ejaculation had been regularly absent for a period of months.

Rarely, some men do climax without ejaculating. This is usually caused by nerve damage that can result from conditions such as diabetes or as a result of surgery. Retrograde ejaculation, when the seminal fluid is released backwards into the bladder, can follow prostate surgery.

Occasional inability to orgasm or ejaculate is often associated with stress, too much alcohol, some recreational drugs, tiredness or lack of desire for any reason. Often, men have a sufficient erection for penetration but they don't actually feel very aroused. Hormonal imbalances, some prescribed drugs – including antidepressants – alcohol and substance misuse can also interfere with the ability to ejaculate in the longer term, though these would generally affect ejaculation from masturbation as well as intercourse.

Confidence

Pain during intercourse can influence the development of inhibited ejaculation, but in many men there are thought to be more psychological reasons. It can begin to occur during periods of stress when you have difficulty in relaxing. It can happen to any man at any time, out of the blue. However, some studies have shown that men who have difficulty in climaxing have sometimes had very little partnered sexual experience, which leads to a lack of confidence and performance anxiety. You may find it difficult to explain your feelings to your partner, so you don't get the reassurance you need to relax enough to orgasm. The more you care about your partner, the more difficult it may be to climax, as you are so concerned about performing well.

Sometimes, partners comment favourably on a man's ability to keep going without climaxing and this positive reinforcement may then make ejaculation seem like failure. Indeed, some men like being unable to climax and don't see it as a problem. It may be that the hormones produced during arousal cause feelings of wellbeing which also reinforce this idea. Moreover, the combination of inadequate sex education and lack of experience lead some men with inhibited ejaculation to have unrealistic expectations of sex and how long they should be able to 'last' before climaxing. Training themselves not to climax may ultimately lead to difficulty in ejaculating, particularly with a partner, and especially if they also have the idea that ejaculating into their partner is dirty or unwelcome. Some men lose their erection during intercourse, as they run out of energy.

Some problems with ejaculation begin in adolescence, particularly for boys who have shared bedrooms or dormitories. Fear of being discovered masturbating leads some boys to try to control ejaculation. Some squeeze their penis as they climax so that the ejaculate seeps out, rather than spurting, and this seepage effect can become habitual. Because this is unusual, orgasm may be avoided while with a partner, though this may not be a conscious decision.

Trying to orgasm quickly before discovery leads many boys to develop an excellent technique, involving a firm grip and rapid manipulation. Sex with partners is then rarely as effective and may be disappointing. In straight couples, this issue may only begin after a partner has had a baby and her vagina feels less tight. Experimenting with different positions may alleviate this somewhat. Entering from behind, with the woman's legs together, may provide a snug effect, for instance, particularly when lying side to side. However, you may be one of many men who are reluctant to discuss your needs in case you hurt your partner's feelings, or you may feel you shouldn't bother your partner with what you see as just your problem. However, in common with all sexual problems, this is a shared issue. Until your partner understands you feel there is a difficulty, they won't be able to help or reassure you. Sometimes, it can be such a relief that your partner knows how you feel that this alone is enough to start making things better.

Pornography

Using a lot of pornography can also lead to ejaculatory issues, especially if you have difficulty in fantasising while with your partner. It isn't just that the idealised images from porn give an unrealistic idea of partnered sex, though this can undoubtedly happen, but the quick route to arousal and orgasm offered by visual images trains the brain to need this stimuli. Coupled with the perfect masturbatory technique, it is no wonder that porn users often find sex with their partners unsatisfactory. There is more about this in Chapter Eight, *Sexual Secrets* (see pages 107–24).

Feeling that fantasy during sex with their partner is some kind of betrayal prevents some men from using it to help arouse them. As the section on fantasy explains (see page 227), this is not the case. On the contrary, as the end result is satisfying sex with your partner, it is to be encouraged.

Partners

If you are the partner of someone with inhibited ejaculation, you may have experienced a mixture of emotions about this. You may feel that your partner would climax if you were more attractive, for instance, or you may feel you should be doing more to excite him. But, as we have seen, there are numerous causes for inhibited ejaculation which have nothing to do with desire or attraction. A very common trigger is a single incident of difficulty with ejaculation, often due to tiredness or heavy drinking, which worries the man enough to cause longer-term performance anxiety. There tend to be general expectations that men should 'last' during intercourse – but not too long. As the duration of most penetrative lovemaking is only about two or three minutes, a long delay in climaxing is likely to be noticeable. However, there is also a general expectation that women's attempts to orgasm may be protracted, and that this should be tolerated. Bearing this in mind, women with partners who are slow to climax should try not to criticise, as this will only increase anxiety.

If both of you are frightened to discuss this, it could go on indefinitely, probably becoming worse. Meanwhile, you may both be experiencing soreness and bruising from the excessive thrusting. It can be difficult to know when to stop, and who initiates giving up can be as problematic as who initiates sex in the first place.

More men than might be expected – given the evidence of no ejaculate and an erection – solve the problem by faking their orgasm. The whole business can become mechanical and end up feeling anything but sensual, loving, erotic or arousing. Often, the problem is not addressed until such time as you decide to start a family. Alternatively, inhibited ejaculation may be provoked in some men by worries about the responsibility for making their partner pregnant or by fear of parenthood.

Pelvic exercises

In common with orgasmic disorders affecting women, it is possible that some men have difficulty in letting go, particularly if they value self-control in their everyday lives. Removing stress, becoming more relaxed with your partner, drinking less and counselling are all ways of approaching the issue. Sometimes, learning to relax and ignore intrusive thoughts – perhaps by practising mindfulness techniques – is enough to make orgasm more attainable. You can also learn to control the muscles concerned with relaxing to ejaculate so that you are better able to do so during intercourse.

The pubococcygeus (PC) muscle exists in both sexes and extends from the pubic bone to the coccyx, acting like a hammock to support the pelvic organs. It is relaxed both during ejaculation and while passing urine. Therefore, it can be located by stopping the flow in the middle of a wee. Noting the physical process of relaxing and contracting the PC muscle when you pass urine can help you learn to practise doing this when you aren't weeing too. Attempting this several times a day may lead to skilled control which can eventually be used during intercourse.

While the issue of inhibited ejaculation exists, try not to focus on intercourse but on shared sensual and erotic experiences which you both enjoy. This is a chance to extend your sensual and sexual repertoire and spend more time enjoying caressing and stimulation rather than hurrying to intercourse. Indeed, it is a good idea to delay penetration until you are very highly aroused. Try to maintain stimulation during intercourse through deep kissing and genital or anal touch and allow yourself to fantasise. In fact, use whatever stimulates you, but don't make ejaculation your only goal.

Setting out to have a mutually satisfying and loving experience will be more likely to help you relax in the long run. Think about the benefits of a series of wonderfully warm and erotic sessions of sensuality, where orgasm is not the objective, compared with high-stress episodes of ineffective attempts to climax. Most of all, don't keep your concerns to yourself or be victim to the pesky 'oughts', which tell you a real man *ought* to ejaculate at will/satisfy his partner through intercourse/not require stimulation. A problem shared is a problem halved and you can have a lot of fun remedying this together.

Faking orgasm

Though a huge number of both men and women do fake orgasm on occasions, partners are often hurt if they find out. Faking most commonly seems to happen when one of the couple is tired and not particularly aroused, probably making love to please the partner rather than because they felt like it themselves. Indeed, the faking is often done out of consideration for the partner's feelings. You may fake because you don't want to orgasm but your partner wants you to climax. Or you could be frightened of feeling overwhelmed by the orgasm.

Recently, research has shown that many women fake orgasm to increase their arousal and/or as an orgasmic trigger. Partners may be aware of this and it is certainly the case that doing what your body feels like doing is likely to lead to more pleasure than fighting back your natural inclinations.

Difficulty climaxing in women

The absence of orgasm is known as anorgasmia. You may never have had an orgasm (primary anorgasmia) or the problem may be acquired. Many men *and* women expect women to be able to climax during intercourse and think there is something wrong if this does not happen. However, some estimates suggest that fewer than a third of women are regularly able to orgasm through intercourse. It could even be as few as one in ten, suggesting that the vast majority of women find this rarely or never happens.

Even when women do climax during intercourse, it is thought to be caused by direct or indirect stimulation of the clitoris. Therefore, positions which allow clitoral stimulation, such as with the woman on top, or manual stimulation of the clitoris during intercourse, are usually needed to facilitate orgasm.

The psychoanalyst Sigmund Freud is largely responsible for the belief that women should be having so-called 'vaginal orgasms', as he declared they were infinitely preferable to the more immature 'clitoral orgasm'. This idea persists even though it has since been repeatedly shown to be nonsense. The vagina has relatively few nerve endings, whereas the clitoris has up to twice as many as a penis.

Clitoral stimulation

Both the visible clitoris and clitoral tissue present in the vulva and anterior wall of the vagina can be stimulated. Women who have large amounts of clitoral tissue close to the surface of the vagina and vulva are those most likely to experience so-called vaginal orgasms. Other stimulation is accounted for by indirect clitoral touch or bringing the clitoris into contact with something like the pelvic bone. This is very difficult to do in the traditional missionary position, with the man above; on top, women are better able to control clitoral contact. During arousal the clitoris and vulval area become engorged with blood, increasing the possibility of indirect clitoral stimulation.

A great deal has been written about different kinds of female orgasms and about different ways of achieving them. It is true that some women's orgasms are more intense than others at different times and even during the same bout of lovemaking. However, as they are all caused by direct or indirect clitoral stimulation, it doesn't matter whether you can find your G spot, climax during intercourse or orgasm 20 times in a row, finding how that stimulation works for you is crucial. This means being patient, realistic and prepared to experiment.

Some women experience primary anorgasmia and have never been able to climax either with a partner or through masturbation. For many women, though, the anorgasmia follows trauma or childbirth. Sometimes it is related to inhibitions about losing control with a partner or talking with their partner about what stimulates them. Sometimes it is termed 'situational anorgasmia' because it is associated with a particular person or situation, such as oral sex, or only occurs with partnered sex and not masturbation. Ability to climax can also be affected by some medications – especially antidepressants and the contraceptive pill – and clinical conditions, particularly neurological disorders and diabetes. There is more about this in Chapter Ten, *Physical Limitations* (see pages 132–52).

Masturbation is an effective way to discover what turns you on and how your body responds. Get to know your body well, as it changes throughout the menstrual cycle, and you may find your sensitivity changes too. Touch that feels great just after your period can be too intense by mid-month, for instance. If you can orgasm through masturbation, however, there is no reason why you won't climax with your partner. Even if you have been successfully masturbating for years, it is useful to consider what you find particularly arousing, what fantasies or images are especially exciting and what helps you to orgasm. Mindfulness techniques (see pages 43 and 91), which help you to dismiss unwelcome thoughts and focus on the here and now, can be very usefully employed to allow you to focus on your arousal.

Inhibitions

For many women and men, there may be ideas about sex being wrong or dirty, which can inhibit arousal and orgasm, or, equally unhelpfully, there may be a fear of letting go. Indeed, the physical experience of climaxing can be startling if it is unexpected. Rhythmic muscular contractions occur throughout the pelvic and anal area. The vagina and uterus contract in women and the prostate in men as semen is expelled during ejaculation. Some women are simply bothered by the amount of mucus produced when they are aroused and actively try to lessen their arousal as a result (more about this on page 103).

Some men and women arch their back, curl up their toes or grimace as they orgasm, and it is these involuntary responses which worry some of us, particularly if we fear we will look silly. However, partners usually have their own look to worry about, hopefully being more involved in their own orgasm than concerned about silly faces. Many people automatically close their eyes when they are very aroused in any case and the throes of passion are more often perceived as sexy rather than silly.

Fear of feeling overwhelmed by the sensation of orgasm is common, or that some physical embarrassment will occur, such as farting, weeing, screaming or crying. In the unlikely event that you did any of those, partners could be delighted that you were so overcome by the experience. On balance, they are more likely to be pleased that you have orgasmed at all rather than worrying about anything else that might happen. Physical disasters – as you might see them – are less common than you would imagine.

Orgasmic triggers

Some psychosexual therapists suggest pretending you are having an orgasm when you are on your own so that you have the experience of letting rip in your own way when there is no one around to make you feel inhibited. When this is transferred to lovemaking, partners often find it very exciting – though beware of faking orgasm to please your partner in case it becomes regularly required. Recent research has shown that pretending to orgasm really is often the trigger needed to make it happen.

Other triggers to orgasm may be activities like arching your back or curling your toes, tensing and relaxing, screaming or thrashing around. I often suggest that my clients spend the day at a theme park riding roller coasters together so they have the opportunity to scream and let off steam. It is surprising how often this shared activity later leads to more relaxation during lovemaking and the ability to allow orgasmic triggers to progress, rather than avoiding the final trip over into ecstasy.

If you have not yet orgasmed, you may want to try it alone first if you are worried about your response. If your problem is worrying about what will happen when you orgasm, this is all the more reason to practise by yourself so that you know what to expect. Spending relaxed time touching your breasts and genitals, as well as discovering other erogenous zones such as the inner thighs, and noticing what you find arousing, is important so that you can take responsibility for your own orgasm. Expecting your partner to 'make' you climax takes away your own control and means you have no way of achieving orgasm by yourself. Also, you can't know how to show, guide, advise or ask your partner for whatever stimulates you if you don't know yourself. You can experiment with erotic literature, pictures or film, develop your own fantasies – anything that you enjoy.

Bear in mind that millions and millions of people do survive orgasm every single day, so whatever loss of control you fear can't be that bad. For example, if you know that you always burst into tears when you orgasm – and a few people do – just warn your partner that it is part of the experience for you, no biggie.

Vibrators

Once you are used to a little arousal, a vibrator may help to move things along. These are available online as well as in stores and there is a huge range to choose from. Many women are put off by the idea of huge dildos which are often the focus of jokes about vibrators. However, modern devices come in all shapes and sizes, from a vibrating rubber duck for bath-time play to mini vibrators which fit in a handbag. Others are designed to fit over your hand for massage of the mons or general vulval area if you prefer less intense and direct stimulation. Experimenting with touch and pressure is essential to find what suits you. Alternatively, some women enjoy the effects produced by a well-directed jet of water – but *never* douche or aim water into the vagina, particularly using a high-pressure shower.

Some people continue to experience orgasm, but the pleasure which used to be associated with it disappears. This is sometimes due to hormone changes, stress, distress or to over-tightening the pelvic-floor muscles as orgasm approaches, thereby inhibiting the waves of contraction associated with climax.

If any of these problems persist, or you feel you need help from the outset, it is worth seeking medical advice and consulting a psychosexual therapist. What to expect from psychosexual therapy is explained in the following chapter.

Chapter Twelve
Psychosexual Therapy

There are many misconceptions about the nature of psychosexual therapy (PST). Some people think they are going to have hands-on lessons in sexual techniques in the therapy room, which may involve sex with their partner or even the therapist (known as sexual surrogacy). However, though they may teach techniques such as relaxation and mindfulness, no UK psychosexual therapists touch their clients sexually and exercises are always conducted in the privacy of your own home.

Some of the misunderstandings have probably arisen thanks to films and TV programmes about early sex researchers and therapists, such as *Kinsey, A Dangerous Method* and *Masters of Sex,* as well as some lurid media accounts about unregulated sexual coaching. In the UK, modern psychosexual therapy requires a high level of training and experience; for instance, many Relate psychosexual therapists study to masters level. Many of these are also members of the psychosexual therapists' professional organisation, the College of Sexual and Relationship Therapists (COSRT), which keeps a directory the public can check to find a qualified therapist. More experienced therapists can apply to COSRT for accreditation. Relate's psychosexual therapy diploma is also accredited by COSRT.

The very early sex therapists provided information and education at a time when sex wasn't talked about and most people were largely uninformed. Since then, sex education has become available to everyone in the Western world, both in school and via the media. Therefore, modern *psycho*sexual therapists are interested in the way couples think and feel as well as their bedroom behaviour, so their treatment programmes are designed to improve sexual outcomes through behavioural exercises *and* changes in thinking.

CASE EXAMPLE: RITA AND LIM

When Rita and Lim eventually approached a psychosexual therapist, they had been experiencing problems for more than a decade. The couple, in their forties, had two school-aged children and both worked full-time, so they had very little spare energy or time for their sexual relationship. They had only been making love once or twice a year for several years and there was little physical contact overall. Now the children were older, they had a little more space and wanted to be more intimate, but they didn't know how to restart a more regular sex life. They both thought Rita was less interested in sex than Lim.

The therapist took a detailed history from each of them and discovered that neither came from a family which was comfortable talking about sex and that both were relatively sexually inexperienced when they met – factors which made it more difficult for them to discuss and resolve sexual issues. Rita revealed that, though she could orgasm easily through masturbation, this happened very rarely during sex with Lim. Lim, meanwhile, worried that he climaxed too quickly and agreed that he would like to learn ways to improve his ejaculatory control.

During a three-way discussion with the therapist following the history-taking and assessment sessions,

Lim blurted out that he had never felt he could satisfy Rita despite his deep desire and longing to make love to her. Rita was astonished. The therapist pointed out that they both seemed sexually shy and had never found a way to comfortably communicate either their sexual needs or their feelings about each other. They agreed goals to improve their communication, to achieve more regular and satisfying sexual experiences together, along with better ejaculatory control for Lim and more orgasms for Rita if and when she wanted them.

The therapist developed a treatment plan which involved both individual and joint exercises for the couple, initially aimed at increasing their sensual awareness and feelings of connection. They loved all the exercises and surprised the therapist by overcoming their shyness and hesitancy at an early stage. They found themselves becoming aroused by the touching exercises and feeling very close so they were eager to move on to more sexually focused exercises while retaining their new sense of connection. Though they were very anxious about deliberately trying to become aroused, they took things slowly and their progress went well so that they were soon able to introduce some of their individual exercises into the couple sessions and help one another with these. The therapist gave them information about sexual responsiveness, which helped them to focus less on achieving orgasms during intercourse and more on having a sexual experience which was intimate and satisfying. As it turned out, satisfying intercourse became a part of this but no longer felt like the most important part. Rita was orgasming successfully during sexual encounters with Lim and Lim felt much more in control of when he would ejaculate.

CASE EXAMPLE: STELLA AND PATRICK

Stella and Patrick, who were in their late fifties, had enjoyed a very successful sexual relationship until the year or so before they presented for psychosexual therapy. In their joint assessment session, they both said that their only problem was that Patrick was having increasing difficulty achieving and maintaining an erection. However, during the individual history-taking sessions it emerged that Stella was deeply worried that Patrick no longer found her attractive and that his difficulty maintaining an erection reflected this. Patrick was also very worried that Stella did not find him attractive. He felt he had put on weight, was losing his hair and felt tired all the time. He was also worried that he would never be able to 'perform properly' sexually again, as he rarely had erections in the morning, produced very little ejaculate when he climaxed and didn't really feel very interested in sex, though he pretended to. He admitted to the therapist that he had been secretly buying Viagra from the internet, but it hadn't worked.

The therapist thought the couple needed some information about the normal process of ageing and help to boost their sexual confidence together, but she felt that consulting his GP was a priority for Patrick. He was embarrassed and reluctant to do this, but the therapist explained that the problems he had been experiencing were very common and there might be an easily treatable explanation for them. At the very least, she urged him to put his mind at rest that nothing was seriously wrong.

As it turned out, Patrick had low testosterone levels which *were* easily treatable and the GP also prescribed a similar drug to Viagra to help him until his testosterone levels returned to normal. The couple continued with the psychosexual therapy during this time to try to improve their communication and allow them to reconnect. The therapist set non-sexual touching exercises to begin with to help the couple relearn their physical connection without the pressure and anxiety which they associated with sex. Though they struggled with these to begin with, as they both wanted to get back to having regular intercourse, they quickly began to appreciate their new sense of connectedness and to really enjoy this special time. Patrick also practised exercises to get back his erection when he lost it, which the couple incorporated into their lovemaking. Stella recognised that Patrick's loss of erection was nothing to do with her attractiveness – indeed, the therapy made them feel closer and sexier than ever.

WHAT TO EXPECT

Arranging to see a psychosexual therapist may feel daunting. You are planning to talk to a stranger about the most private and potentially sensitive aspects of your life. It may also be something you have been thinking about for a while and having it up your sleeve as a possibility may have been comforting. Once you actually start, it may feel as though this is your last chance – as if everything is depending on this working – and that can be scary.

Initial assessment

The therapist will do their best to put you at ease. Sometimes one partner has an initial meeting to find out about the PST process. However, you may prefer to attend as a couple to see whether PST would be suitable for you. Either way, this is an opportunity for you to ask questions as well as for the therapist to ascertain what problems you have been experiencing. Finding out more also allows you to see whether you have the time for the process or whether it may be better to wait until your life is less busy. Sometimes issues like a medical or mental-health problem, drug or alcohol issues, may make it difficult to engage with therapy, or there may be other relationship problems which need to be addressed first.

You don't need to be in a relationship to receive PST, and many individuals are successfully treated, but it can be helpful to see couples together – rather than just the partner with 'the problem' – because both of you will be affected by what has been happening. What's more, it may be easier to introduce your individual learning to your lovemaking when your partner has been part of the process all along. Performance anxiety is not so likely to crop up when you are only performing for yourself, for instance. Psychosexual therapy can be enjoyable for both of you too. Couples offer one another considerable encouragement and usually feel the PST process deepens their overall relationship as well as improving their sex life.

History taking

If, after the initial assessment, it seems appropriate to proceed, individual meetings will be held with each of you to get to know you in much more depth and try to work out why and how the problem is affecting you. People generally enjoy these meetings, which don't turn out to be anything like as daunting as might be expected. It is helpful to be as honest as you can and think about anything that is troubling you or you need to explain so that this can be effectively managed during therapy; you can always tell the therapist if there is anything that you really don't want to share with your partner.

Before proceeding, the therapist may suggest visiting your GP if you haven't already done so, to rule out clinical causes. Even if a medical reason is found, however, PST is often still very helpful, especially when anxiety is having an effect on the relationship.

Making goals

With the information that has been gathered, the therapist will devise a treatment plan to meet your particular needs. This may include some exercises which are similar to those mentioned earlier in the book or different ones which are more suitable for you. This will be discussed at a meeting of all three of you, where you will learn how and why this particular plan has been developed for you. As well as personal considerations, religious and cultural influences may need to be factored in, and your input about this is encouraged and appreciated.

Couples usually find these meetings absolutely fascinating, as they summarise their experiences and offer a way forward. The meeting is meant to be a three-way discussion, so there will always be plenty of opportunity to chip in with your ideas. Together with the therapist, you will make some realistic goals for the work – if, that is, you all agree it would be beneficial to continue.

Treatment

Neither the goals nor the treatment plan are set in stone. In fact, a key facet of PST is that it is so adaptable, responding to your experience and new information or thinking as it occurs. The therapist may set individual and couple exercises for you right away, to be done about three times a week at home; these exercises will usually be sensual rather than sexual to begin with in order to shed old habits and remove any performance pressure associated with sex. You will then report back to the therapist at regular meetings, usually every week or fortnight. Finding time for the exercises can be challenging in itself. This may demonstrate to you how difficult it has been to fit lovemaking into your busy lives.

It is also likely that there will be some relevant sex education, mindfulness or relaxation exercises, pelvic-floor exercises and thinking exercises. The therapist wants as much information as possible in order to help set the next exercise, so the appointments to give feedback are your chance to honestly say how they went. You probably just want the exercise to go well; of course, the therapist will be pleased for you if it does. If it doesn't, however, it is helpful to think of the exercises as experiments. Whether they go well or not, it's a win-win situation, as problems you report give the therapist more information to work with to help find long-term solutions to your issues. It is almost inevitable that the therapy will meet a block at some point, so don't be disheartened if you hit a brick wall. This can be what ends up leading to the greatest improvement.

Maintenance

The length of therapy is extremely variable, with some people experiencing a big difference in only a few sessions while others take longer, often relishing the process. However long it takes, it is hoped that you will emerge with a toolbox of strategies and ideas to keep you going indefinitely. Of course, you can always come back if you get stuck; a follow-up appointment is usually offered after three to six months to see how you are getting along. This allows time for any remaining glitches to emerge and for you to build confidence by yourselves. It is truly remarkable to see the difference in wellbeing and self-assurance in couples between their first meeting and the follow-up, which is often extremely celebratory.

In the same spirit, the next part of the book looks at ways of celebrating your sexuality and relationship and keeping the sexual magic alive, as well as recognising some of the pitfalls you may encounter going forward.

Part Four
Maintaining and Improving Your Sex Life

Chapter Thirteen
Sexual Realism

Babies cry, parents get sick, you're short of cash, you have work problems, you argue about housework, the children leave home. You are under pressure from all directions ... Life happens. However, it is often your relationship that is blamed when other stuff is affecting it. Your relationship is probably the one constant part of your life, so it is always going to be affected by other factors and events that you are going through. It is very easy, therefore, to think that the relationship is the problem, rather than all the other pressures which are affecting the relationship. When you are under pressure, sex in your relationship is often an early casualty. If this worries you, you may increase your concern by regretting that you aren't having the kind of sex you enjoyed when you first met.

However, we have already seen how the excitement of the early days, and the influence of attachment hormones, help us to forget any initial problems. We also know that the early connection with our partners is biologically focused on bonding. If relationships remained as exciting and befuddling as they are at the beginning we would never be able to get on with our lives. Later in our relationship, we are programmed to experience partner connection in a calmer, less intense way. This allows us to maintain the relationship, take care of one another and raise our families.

FIRE-FIGHTING PROBLEMS

We aren't, as a rule, aware that an element of tedium helps to keep us together. For no good reason, we may believe relationships should remain passionate and exciting. If the early excitement has blinded us to real relationship difficulties or incompatibility, we may have deliberately continued to avoid addressing these as they became evident, hoping longevity would sort them out. This is particularly common where sexual issues are concerned, as familiarity is often expected to somehow fix any problems. This is understandable, but hope alone does not help partners to be honest about their needs, which can become lost as time passes.

The more romance recedes and humdrum normality takes over, the easier it is to focus on relationship difficulties. However, the alternative is to put time and effort into creating circumstances which make it simpler to see issues coming and tackle them together. Admittedly, this is easier said than done when you are busy and exhausted. Instead, you may get used to fire-fighting relationship problems as they arise. Blaming your partner and wishing they would change may be your default response, rather than working on what you each need to help you develop as an individual and as one half of a couple. This is difficult, as it means taking responsibility for yourself and your contribution to the relationship, rather than just wishing for something different.

If you base the strength of your relationship on sexual frequency alone, or consider it a major sign of troubles, you may not notice the skills and strengths you have been developing along the way. Even if sexual encounters are relatively rare, over the years you have probably successfully tackled all sorts of crises together and enjoyed all manner of successes. This is positive evidence about your relationship, but are you willing to pay attention to it?

Looking for alternatives

If you think about a recent argument or dissatisfied feeling, consider what made you behave the way you did. Was this a knee-jerk reaction or a considered response following a careful weighing up of the pros and cons of your actions balanced against the potential outcome?

CASE EXAMPLE: LIV AND ULRIKA

Liv doesn't see infrequent sex as affecting the quality of her relationship with Ulrika. However, Liv *does* think pestering indicates a relationship problem, and this makes her more likely to refuse sex. Liv hasn't considered the effect that refusing sex has on Ulrika.

Ulrika sees sex as the most important sign that the relationship is okay. Consequently, she pesters Liv for sex without realising that Liv sees this as a sign that the relationship is in trouble.

Ulrika worries that the relationship is in trouble.

She pesters Liv for sex to reassure herself.

Liv sees this as a sign the relationship is in trouble and so refuses sex.

Liv and Ulrika's situation is an example of walking around obstacles rather than dealing with them.

When couples say they have tried everything to fix a problem, what they usually mean is that they have done the same thing over and over again. So if you see sex as an indicator of relationship health, pestering for sex is pointless when you know the response to pestering is always refusal. In the end, you probably just give up. Instead, you could look at alternatives to pestering, such as wooing, having a conversation about how you manage sex and intimacy, seeking your partner's opinion about alternative ways to initiate sex, going on holiday or assessing the evidence for other factors affecting the relationship and how these are managed.

Walking around obstacles

When both of you think only of your own needs and feelings, you don't even notice how the behaviour reinforces negative thinking. If your partner doesn't want sex because the relationship doesn't feel right, making them have sex won't fix it. If your partner pesters for sex to make the relationship feel right, refusal won't stop them. Furthermore, if either or both of you are having sex just to tick the box, the chances are that it won't be anything like as much fun as it could be. Yet this almost inevitably happens when you are both focusing on the request for sex rather than the sex itself.

Do look at more than just the request when you decide to refuse or agree to sex. For example, many couples find their relationship improves in the day or so after they've made love and this is a powerful motivator. It is also probably the case that, at some point in their lives, most adults in close relationships have chosen to make love when they didn't really want to or were feeling too tired. The list of reasons for having sex in Chapter Four (see page 62) demonstrates the many factors which may be involved in the decision. It is much more complex than popular culture leads us to believe.

The simplistic need–satisfaction dynamic may seem so normal partly because sex research traditionally examined sex in laboratory subjects, which produced a very linear, one-dimensional description of sexual response:

Arousal – Plateau – Orgasm – Resolution

Real-life lovemaking rarely follows such a simple cycle. Arousal may ebb and flow, and many individuals reach the plateau phase of high excitement, which occurs just before orgasm, and then return to an earlier stage of arousal. Many men do this deliberately, for instance, to prolong lovemaking (also see pages 168–69). Though 'desire' was later added to the sexual-response cycle, to precede arousal, the two are often confused. For many people, desire *follows* arousal and the decision to make love is pragmatic, a weighing up of the pros and cons.

FINDING TIME FOR SEX

Insistence on sexual spontaneity often means never having sex because the circumstances and desire never coincide. For some couples who enter sex therapy, finding or making time for sensuality and lovemaking is one of the most important aspects of the whole process. It may be that you genuinely don't have time to make love or that you are missing some great opportunities. Similarly, if you think that your sex life has become stale or boring, consider what is stopping you from doing something different.

EXERCISE: MAKING CHANGES

Think about an area of your life that you would like to change. It could be how you share chores, make time for yourself, organise your day or work, anything.

Break this down into a list of different activities and jot down what you would like to change and what would be your ideal outcome.

Look at the list carefully, seeing if there are any changes you could make to each item right now. Often, the first step is a fairly minor adjustment to your routine.

Think about what is stopping you from doing it. The reason is often one of the following:

➤ You are hoping someone else will do it.
➤ You need to have a conversation with someone about it.
➤ You resent being the one to fix the issue.

You need to decide whether no action will make you feel better than taking some action. Would your life be more pleasant if you did?

If you do make changes, think about how you feel – more in control or more resentful?

Now repeat the exercise looking at your sexual relationship. Take care to look realistically at the possibilities available to you as well as your wishes.

If you are both prepared to think creatively, you may find that there is more you can do to make changes than you think and that inaction just leaves you feeling out of control and aggrieved. Where sex is concerned, it may be that your thinking is influenced by the way you feel things *should* be rather than what is possible. Use the talking point about sexual frequency below to help you consider this. These questions may be difficult. It is far easier to just go along as you have been doing, without thinking too deeply, as any possibility of change is hard. It is, therefore, important to give sufficient time and thought to each question, allowing yourself to consider what *you* want rather than what you think you should want or would please your partner. It is much harder than you might expect to think only of your own needs and not to be distracted by what you think you have to do. It can also be quite a challenge to consider plans for change. This means taking responsibility for your own needs, admitting you have them and being unable to place all the blame on your partner for what has been happening. Though initially tough, this can be incredibly liberating, offering a much greater sense of control.

TALKING POINT: SEXUAL FREQUENCY

➤ How often do you think couples at your age and stage of relationship ought to make love?

➤ What makes you think this?

➤ Do you think this makes you very different to other couples you know?

➤ What sort of frequency would please you?

➤ Would an increase in the non-sexual intimacy in your relationship help to make you feel your needs were being met?

➤ How could you achieve this?

➤ What would help you to feel satisfied with the lovemaking and intimacy in your relationship?

➤ How much of this is influenced by what you feel you ought to be doing as compared with what is possible?

ASEXUAL RELATIONSHIPS

There are times in most relationships when lovemaking may be rare, but you can still feel close and connected so long as you both consciously accept what is happening and monitor this. Commonly, cuddles are avoided in case sex is expected, whereas if you both agree intercourse is not possible at present there is no reason to deny yourselves physical closeness. When circumstances change, you can rediscover lovemaking all over again if you want to.

Drifting into periods which are sexually fallow is almost inevitable, but it is much harder to restart your sexual connection if you don't acknowledge what is going on. Of course, some couples actively choose to end their sexual relationship, either temporarily or permanently, and should feel confident in their decision if this is what they both want. A recognised decision is very different from drifting apart sexually due to lack of motivation, fear or avoidance. Asexual relationships can still involve a great deal of physical contact, closeness and warmth; they may even become closer once sexual pressure is removed.

SEPARATE BEDS

Sometimes, something as simple as hot flushes, farting in bed, snoring or poor hygiene can wreck your sexual connection. There are some personal features which are positively off-putting and the only way to deal with them is to opt for separate beds or even separate bedrooms. Many couples find a 'visit' to the other's bed is much more sexy and enjoyable than a night struggling to sleep or enduring their own or their partner's unwanted nocturnal behaviour. Embarrassment about snoring or night sweats can be just as inhibiting to yourself as they can be annoying to your partner.

If you do sleep separately, there is all the more reason to make sex special when it occurs (more about this on page 86). Scheduling sex offers the dual benefits of anticipation and preparation. You may be able to build up your desire if you know what is coming and you can take turns to play host. You have time, for instance, to warm or air the room, remove any balled-up tissues, light candles, play your favourite music, clean your teeth and have a wash.

HYGIENE

Though there are times when sweaty sex may be appealing, on the whole it is more acceptable to be clean. This isn't about making sure you've had a leg wax before you're prepared to be sexual, despite what magazines would have you believe. It is about feeling good and confident about yourself and not putting off your partner. In many countries, people use a bidet to wash their genitals after opening their bowels. If you don't do this, you may need to find a way to wash before you hop into bed together.

As a daily routine, uncircumcised men *must* retract their foreskin and gently wash both the glans area (head) of the penis and inside the foreskin, using soap and warm water. Not doing so can lead to a build-up of smelly secretions known as smegma (more about this on page 149). Women can be affected too, with smegma build-up around the clitoris and inside the internal labia. Armpits, underneath the breasts or any fatty areas, the belly button, anal area and testicles are all places which can become sweaty, smelly and sore. This can lead to fungal infections – not sexy. Keeping pubic hair trimmed (not necessarily shaved or waxed) also helps to avoid accumulation of urine and secretions. Smelling of cigarette smoke or alcohol, having bad breath or even just wearing overpowering perfume or aftershave can be very offensive to some people. Taking a bath or shower separately or together to relax and scrub up before sex is, consequently, a great routine to develop.

Many couples who think they have sexual problems simply find that a change in their circumstances or routine fixes everything. It could be that a relaxing holiday, away from all the everyday stresses, is all you both need to recover your mojo. This may also offer the time and space you need to talk things over and reconnect. This is important as effective communication is not always easy as Chapter 14 shows.

Chapter Fourteen
Communicating

Couples rarely share the same communication style. If you value talking and disclosure, and find it relatively easy, you may think there is something wrong if you have a partner who prefers to ponder before offering an opinion or who finds talking very difficult. You may even self-disclose more yourself in order to encourage your partner to talk. However, this may end up putting them off, especially if what you say involves complaints or blaming.

Once again, it may seem as though things have changed since you first met. There is often a great deal of talking and storytelling at the beginning of relationships, when you are getting to know each other, and you may miss this. However, there was probably much more to say when you first met and you probably had more time to spend alone together. Early on, you were probably also editing what you said to place yourself in the most attractive light.

Though they do promote intimacy, these early conversations and disclosures are not difficult. It can be very much harder to talk about how you are feeling when you are together every day and there is so much more at stake. Often, it feels as if there is less to lose by confiding in friends or even strangers. Nevertheless, the clearer you are with your partner about what you do and don't want, the more likely you are to get what you want. You may think you are communicating well, but it isn't always the case. Try the following quiz to check your communication style.

QUIZ: HOW YOU COMMUNICATE

1. When you have a problem, who are you most likely to discuss it with?
   a) Your partner
   b) Your partner, family and friends
   c) Depends who could help
   d) None of the above – you would keep it to yourself

2. If there was an issue you wanted to discuss with your partner, would you:
   a) Drop hints and hope your partner guesses what's bothering you?
   b) Blurt it out at the first opportunity?
   c) Arrange a time to have a proper chat?
   d) Talk to someone else first or instead?

3. When you are telling a story or making a point, do you tend to:
   a) Play down the drama and make events sound less exciting or dangerous?
   b) Exaggerate a bit?
   c) Try to tell a good story but make it as accurate as possible?
   d) It depends on the listener's reaction?

4. If your partner disagrees with you, do you feel:
   a) Hurt and maybe unsure?
   b) Angry and possibly a bit rejected?
   c) Interested in their point of view?
   d) Justified in your own viewpoint?

5. If there is something you want or need, are you most likely to:
    a) Hope your partner guesses?
    b) Drop lots of hints, but make demands if they don't respond?
    c) Clearly and politely ask?
    d) Just take what you need if that's possible or try to fix it yourself?

6. How likely are you to argue?
    a) Very unlikely
    b) Very likely – it clears the air
    c) You'll argue if necessary
    d) You try to avoid arguing but occasionally blow up

7. After an argument, do you usually:
    a) Apologise?
    b) Either feel desperately hurt or behave as though nothing happened?
    c) Think about where you go next?
    d) Sulk?

8. Are arguments usually:
    a) All your fault?
    b) Provoked by your partner?
    c) Provoked by misunderstanding?
    d) To be avoided?

9. If your partner wants to leave a conversation or argument, do you:
    a) Just let them go?
    b) Try to make them stay and face the music?
    c) Agree some time out would be helpful?
    d) You would probably be the one to go?

Mostly As

You seem to lack confidence in your own opinions and may put others' needs ahead of your own. Bravely stating clearly what you want and need may help you and your partner to be more in sync. It may also be helpful to think about why it is so important to you that the two of you never disagree. Do you feel that thinking differently threatens the relationship, for instance? If so, consider where that idea comes from. Sometimes, coming from a family where differences were never expressed leads us to believe that something catastrophic could happen if they were. In fact, managing disputes and moving forward helps couples to understand each other even when they continue to disagree.

Mostly Bs

You probably think your partner should be able to read your mind and you may become angry when they can't. You might go along with their views too, but then become frustrated when your needs aren't met. Making your wishes clear in a less roundabout way will probably make life simpler and less volatile.

Mostly Cs

You probably try to be clear and reasonable and pick your arguments depending on what seems worth pursuing. There is a slight danger of trying *too* hard to see the other person's point of view, but you maintain a good balance of communicating and listening on the whole.

Mostly Ds

You probably avoid committing yourself if you can. This may be because you don't want to bother others with your needs, because you are habitually self-sufficient or because you just know you are right. However, you may find your partner would be a little less demanding of you if you were more forthcoming.

SEXUAL CONFIDENCE

Depending on your style of communication, you may have managed pinch points, everyday routine and your sexual relationship without any negotiation at all. Perhaps you just found a way to adjust to one another without talking. If you do talk, you may be one of the many couples who hurry conversations about sex. You may find them embarrassing or be afraid of hearing something critical and hurtful. You may also fear being asked to do something sexual that you don't like or aren't confident about. Again, this is something that shouldn't be hidden.

It is natural for sexual confidence to ebb and flow. Not acknowledging this and avoiding discussing it can turn the relationship into a battleground. If you are each attempting to approach or avoid what you do or don't want, you will find yourselves constantly in defensive positions. Think about what is stopping you from risking honesty. If you feel it makes you vulnerable, be aware that partners often respond much better to vulnerability than to defensiveness. Vulnerability is not to be confused with excessive neediness; in fact, the ability to show vulnerability suggests control, awareness and candour.

SOULMATES

Couples who feel they are soulmates often have the greatest difficulty in acknowledging difference in one another. They are forced to defer to each other to demonstrate their sameness and as a single unit they both avoid vulnerability. For some couples, it may not be each other's comments or criticisms which create distress but *beliefs* about what the other partner thinks, which may be quite mistaken. Similarly, if you expect your partner to mind-read, you are setting yourself up for repeated, and unnecessary, disappointment.

Soulmates don't usually check out each other's beliefs and might be surprised at what they would discover if they were able to put aside their usual ways of relating and try a different approach. However, you may need to have a discussion about how to have your missing conversations. For instance, it is rarely a good idea to initiate a conversation about sex while you're in the middle of lovemaking. If you want to talk about sex, it can sometimes be less threatening to do so when you are both dressed. You could use the talking point on discussing sex below to get you started.

TALKING POINT: DISCUSSING SEX

➤ Which of you feels more comfortable talking about sex? How do you account for this?

➤ Based on past experience, where do you feel more comfortable talking? At home? In a restaurant? Dressed? Naked?

➤ Do you have a sexual language which you both understand? Do you understand when one of you is verbally expressing an interest in sex, for instance? How comfortable are you with sexual words or with

---

> swearing? How is intimacy conveyed? Do you ever feel baffled by what your partner is saying?
> ➤ Are you happiest using clinical terms, colloquial expressions or slang when you talk about sex?
> ➤ Do you have pet names for each other or for body parts?
> ➤ Do you come from families where sex was discussed?
> ➤ How able are you to discuss sex with your children?
> ➤ When you talk about sex together, do you focus on what works or are you mainly critical?

Though it is important to pay attention to *what* is said, and the more subtle aspects of communication, you could take the bull by the horns and talk about *how* you discuss things and how you each know what the other means. The talking point above shows that this is less straightforward than you might imagine. We make meaning by using our experience to help us understand. Consequently, we can miss meaning very easily. How you have a conversation may need to include ways to check meaning and ensure you understand each other. Many couples use their conversations to shed responsibility and blame the other for what is troubling them. This may be because you don't feel in control or are very anxious, but it isn't helpful in moving along your understanding or making changes. In fact, it keeps things stuck in the same old rut. The quiz above helps you to notice your style and its effects, and you may be able to see more clearly which aspects of your communication are and are not helpful.

It may help to think about your response to each of the questions, share this with your partner and discuss whether they have noticed this about you. They may have some ideas about how you could communicate differently and you may also have some insights you could explore with them. From here, it may be much easier to identify what you could change in ways that would help you both to discuss sex more easily.

The exercise below may also be challenging. Identifying words you use for sex or body parts may seem easy to begin with, but it can be a different matter to use them aloud, depending on who you are talking to.

EXERCISE: DISCUSSING SEX

Make a list of all the words and phrases you can possibly think of to describe sexual body parts and sexual acts.

Then list which of these you would use in the following situations.

➤ Talking to your doctor
➤ Talking to family
➤ Talking to friends
➤ Talking to children
➤ Talking to your partner
➤ While making love

It may be interesting to notice which of these you find easiest and most difficult, and why. See if your partner feels the same way and consider what would help you to talk to them more easily.

It will probably become clear when completing this exercise that you don't talk to your partner in the same way that you talk to others. Perhaps you may decide that the way you talk to each other could be more loving or more appropriate to a couple relationship so that you are more able to evolve the sexual language that works for you. Using some of your learning from the discussing sex talking point on page 206 may be an additional aid to your understanding and planning.

THE 'I WANT–I WILL' BOOK

If you find it impossible to talk to one another or to make requests without becoming embarrassed or angry, you may prefer to avoid verbal conversation where possible and make use of an 'I want–I will' book. This can be any old exercise book or a beautiful volume especially bought for the purpose. It should be placed somewhere that will make it easy for you both to look at the book once or twice a day. The idea is that one page contains requests, of what one of you wants, while the opposite page contains the response. The response may just be 'I will think about that' or 'I will talk to you about that before dinner tomorrow' – but there must be a response which begins with the words *I will*. Both of you need to be fully engaged with this process for it to work, so that not only one of you is writing the 'I wants', and to agree not to use the book as a place for criticism, though it can be used to make positive comments. The entries don't have to be just about sex; they can be about anything.

On the next page is an example. Another way to ensure regular communication is with daily checking in. This can be at any time of day but may be a pleasant way to say goodnight. Once again, this is not an excuse to complain, though it may be a time to bring up concerns and arrange when to discuss them. The idea is to very briefly connect with one another and let each other know how the relationship is doing.

I want ...	I will ...
<u>Monday.</u> I want you to know that I was a little embarrassed with the way you spoke to me in front of your mother yesterday.	**<u>Monday.</u> I will try not to embarrass you again. I will be grateful if you will tell me what embarrassed you.**
<u>Tuesday.</u> I want you to know how much I appreciate you taking the time to talk to me about the incident with your mother. Thank you.	
<u>Wednesday.</u> I want you to know how much I enjoyed our lovemaking last night.	<u>Wednesday.</u> I will try not to blush too much. I keep thinking about it!
<u>Thursday.</u> I want to make love to you again.	<u>Thursday.</u> I will not be making love tonight, as I have an early start tomorrow. Maybe at the weekend?
<u>Friday.</u> I want to talk to you about booking a regular sex date!	<u>Friday.</u> I will be happy to discuss it over the weekend – but I'm not making any promises.
<u>Saturday.</u> I want to tell you that I think I now agree with you that a regular ime for sex would be a good idea.	**<u>Saturday.</u> I will be ready and waiting tonight, if Saturday suits you.**
<u>Sunday.</u> I want you to know that I was a little disappointed when you got up so early this morning without a cuddle. Last night was great!	<u>Sunday.</u> I will cuddle you when I get back from walking the dog!!

EXERCISE: CHECKING IN

➤ Ideally, you will check in at the same time each day, making this process a part of your regular routine – maybe before you go to sleep.

➤ Initially, one of you will need to ask, 'How are we today?' However, you will quickly become accustomed to just telling one another how things are going, without the need for prompting.

➤ You are not asking about what sort of day your partner has had, whether the traffic was bad, the kids played up or the boss was a nightmare again; this is an opportunity to ask how *the relationship* feels at this moment.

➤ If possible, try to be appreciative and think of something you liked about what your partner did; for example:

> ➤ 'I loved it when you texted me this morning.'
> ➤ 'I really liked it when you stroked my hair while we were watching TV.'
> ➤ 'I appreciated you supporting me over the pocket money issue.'
> ➤ 'I am still feeling warm and connected after we made love last night.'

➤ Try to use 'I' statements rather than starting sentences with 'you', which tends to sound blaming. The intention here is to avoid arguments, not provoke one, particularly at bedtime. If there is something you aren't happy about, try not to be too reproachful; for example:

> ➤ 'We're okay on the whole, but I was a bit upset when you didn't support me over the pocket money.'

> ➤ 'I am not feeling so good about us today; I always feel a bit disconnected from you when you don't call or text.'
>
> ➤ 'I would have liked it if you'd given me a hug when I got in from work.'
>
> ➤ Try to be positive if you respond and avoid being defensive. If you possibly can, just accept what you each say without much elaboration at the time. If you think you should talk about something further, fix another time to do so. Resist the temptation to stay up until the early hours mulling it over. When you do talk, stick to the rules in the exercise on how to have a conversation (see page 217).
>
> ➤ When you have finished checking in, continue with your routine. If it's bedtime, hopefully this will include at least a goodnight kiss.

REMINISCING

Reminiscing can be another way to restore your sense of sexual connection. It doesn't hurt to remind one another of some of your early meetings and what attracted you to each other in the first place. It can be fun to do this together or maybe with your children. They will probably be delighted with (positive) stories about how you decided to have them, pregnancy and their birth, and they will be thrilled with stories about how you met, first dates and falling in love. Even if yours is a blended family, you can include stories which include meeting and getting to know them. On your own together, you can include early sexual memories as well as events and dates. Rather than making unfavourable comparisons with your sex life today, it should be possible to enjoy your memories and even see if there is anything you could, or would want to, realistically incorporate into your current lovemaking.

SAYING NO TO SEX

The most difficult communication you have may be saying no to sex. This is often not handled well due to embarrassment on both sides. Often, one partner just pushes the other away rather than explaining why or softening the rejection. A conversation about ways to manage this can only be helpful. There is no reason to be unpleasant or aggressive; offering or accepting refusal with a real hug rather than a metaphorical push just makes for a more pleasant relationship.

ASPERGER SYNDROME

Some people have particular difficulty in communicating effectively and appreciating subtleties of meaning. Asperger syndrome is a condition of perception and social behaviour affecting about 1 in 100 people, with males outnumbering females at the rate of about 4:1. Also sometimes described as high-functioning autism spectrum disorder, Asperger syndrome can result in more social awkwardness in affected individuals than in unaffected, neurotypical (NT) people. As a result, they often have difficulty 'reading' others, understanding social niceties or multitasking. They can perceive ideas very literally and have difficulty in following subtle suggestions or in understanding sarcasm or irony. As a result, NT partners can be infuriated with their lack of empathy and insensitivity.

A particular problem can be their obsessions or interests, which are all-consuming. At the beginning of new relationships, the current obsession can often be the partner or sex. This is obviously more than fine, as it makes partners feel extremely special and wanted. When this passion wanes, however, partners are often dismayed and confused, if not downright angry. This may happen after a few months or years or be triggered by another interest, such as wedding planning, a new job or a new baby. The NT partner feels rejected; the Asperger partner doesn't understand why. This is thought to be because they are using the areas of the brain which are logical, rather than interpretive, when they are trying to understand others. This can be infuriating to partners if they don't understand the reasons for the Asperger partner being so emotionally detached and apparently uncaring.

Asperger syndrome and sexual problems

Sexual problems are common, as those affected find it more difficult to create and respond to relationship intimacy. They may not notice sexual cues or necessarily be particularly aware of, or sensitive to, their partner's sexual needs. There may be difficulty responding to change, so lovemaking can become very repetitive. Sensory sensitivity may mean that they are particularly affected by touch, taste and smell. Consequently, they may dislike oral sex, or the lightest touch may mark their skin. Alternatively, they may be particularly *in*sensitive to sensory stimulus, finding it hard to become sufficiently aroused to orgasm.

Use of flavoured dental dams (a square of latex or silicone) may help overcome aversion to oral sex if that is desired (see page 224). Sensate focus exercises (see pages 85–90) can help to determine the kind of touch which is most arousing without damaging the skin. Combined with mindfulness exercises (see pages 43 and 91), they can also help to heighten sensory awareness considerably.

If you think you or your partner could be affected by Asperger syndrome, it may be difficult to decide whether to seek medical assessment. If you are reading this as someone with an Asperger diagnosis, you are almost certainly well aware of having struggled with relationship subtleties, such as flirting and romance, and the complexity this can create. For many people, finding out that there has been a reason for their difficulty comes as a huge relief. Others, however, dislike the idea of being labelled and resist a diagnosis even though some people may think they could be affected. This, in itself, can be enough to create relationship problems.

Partners

For partners, a reason for relationship difficulties can be very reassuring. If you are an NT partner, you may find it easier to cope once you have some answers. Sometimes neither of you may want to have anything to do with a medical label because you believe a diagnosis will end your hope. It is true that it isn't possible to cure Asperger syndrome, but it *is* possible to improve relationships significantly once you both know what you are dealing with. Moreover, people with Asperger syndrome generally respond magnificently to sex therapy, usually being hugely enthusiastic and enjoying the process. Indeed, it often becomes the latest interest.

COMMUNICATING WITH AND WITHOUT WORDS

The following exercises, intended for all couples, look at the way we communicate through conversation and the way meaning making can occur without speech. The first exercise may be more challenging for couples affected by Asperger syndrome, as it deals with such abstract concepts. The second exercise on how to have a conversation may be easier to follow.

EXERCISE: THE SOUNDS OF SILENCE

Silence can communicate a great deal, as this exercise demonstrates.

➤ Sit comfortably, relax and close your eyes.
➤ What can you hear? Whatever it is, it will give clues about where you are and what is happening around you.

   The same is true when nobody is speaking.

   Often we draw conclusions from silences and then react to them without checking out what they *really* mean.
➤ During the next day or so, pay attention to silences and try to decide what they convey. If your partner is around, you could ask what they thought was happening in the silences too.

   Examples could include:

   ➤ A friendly silence
   ➤ A hostile silence
   ➤ A sensual silence
   ➤ A sleepy silence
   ➤ A resentful silence
   ➤ A stunned silence
➤ Try to work out how you know what each silence means. Do you ever get it wrong?
➤ How helpful are each of the silences to your relationship?
➤ Which of them set the scene for sex?
➤ Which close down sexual opportunities?

The silences exercise may make a helpful talking point. It could be useful in revealing what ways you agree and differ in your understanding of silences and whether this surprises either of you. Managing silences can be surprisingly difficult. They can, for instance, be companionable and loving or deeply awkward, hostile or sad. Indeed, your understanding of non-verbal communication may affect the way you approach tricky topics. Silences aren't something we tend to think about very much but the exercise may help you to notice how they can affect your mood and understanding without you even realising. Misunderstanding can easily result when one of you is more comfortable with silence than the other. For example, one of you may enjoy a quiet beginning to the day while the other thinks a silent start is a sign of sulking. As with the other exercises, these questions are tricky but tackling them and talking about them will give you valuable information to help you communicate better.

There are some ideas about communication which help everyone and they are especially useful to follow when life is at its most hectic. When you're both busy, finding the best way to talk isn't always easy. The following exercise contains some ideas of ways to make the most of a discussion.

EXERCISE: HOW TO HAVE A CONVERSATION

➤ **Pick your moment** – plan the conversation for a time when you will both be unhurried and know what to expect rather than blurting everything out when your partner is distracted.

➤ **Determine the purpose of the conversation** – is this banter, a serious talk, information gathering, self-disclosure …?

➤ **Listen as well as speak** – don't use the time when your partner is speaking to plan what you are going to say next.

➤ **Think before you speak** – reflect on what has just been said rather than responding with what you always say or the message you wanted to convey.

➤ **Notice** – couples need to pay attention to what the other is doing or saying, as well as what you imagine they do or say or the scenario in your head.

➤ **Understand** – if your partner offers a reason for something you are complaining about, don't just dismiss it as this may be all you need to know to see things differently.

➤ **Recognise** – when your partner concedes a point or agrees with you, do show you heard and appreciate this; for example, 'I'm glad you said that, because I feel the same way' or 'I know that can't have been easy for you, but it is a huge relief for me'.

➤ **Be direct** – headline statements are much more useful than sideways approaches, which can be misunderstood; for example, 'I would like us to go to my sister's party on Saturday' rather than 'What were you thinking of doing on Saturday?'

➤ **Use 'I' statements** – avoid accusations and own what you want to say; for example 'I feel hurt when you don't call me in the day' is much less blaming than 'You never call' or 'You can never be bothered to call me'.

➤ **Be appreciative** – for example, 'I love it when you call me during the day'.

➤ **Speak quietly** – try to avoid raising your voice, even if your partner does.

> ➤ **Be civil** – avoid swearing, name calling and don't insult your partner or their family members and friends.
> ➤ **Ask** – if you aren't clear about something, calmly ask for clarification. However, don't tell the other person that you know what they say is not what they mean; this disqualifies their feelings and you may well be wrong anyway.
> ➤ **Be original** – don't keep repeating the same thing; the reply won't change.
> ➤ **End on time** – the optimum time for a conversation is just under 20 minutes, so finish well within half an hour and schedule another conversation if the issue is unresolved.
> ➤ **Follow up** – check with your partner how things are going but don't keep pestering for reassurance; for example, 'I had a great time on Saturday night. I hope it was okay for you too' is better than 'You didn't enjoy Saturday, did you?' or 'Please tell me you enjoyed Saturday – what did you like about it?'

If you have the time, it is well worth monitoring how these conversations go and what works best for you. Using the exercise, notice the effect on both of you of what you say and how you say it. What brings out the best in you both? See what changes when you slip back to your old way of conversing and which aspects you particularly want to keep or avoid. Which way is more efficient? Sometimes the efficiency of the conversation is not what couples want; some enjoy the opportunity to criticise one another and lose this when they adopt the exercise above. Therefore, consider your agenda and what you hope to achieve. Simply realising that you are using every conversation as an opportunity to blame may help you to stop or to work out why this is happening. Adopting a more useful way of having a discussion should make blame unnecessary.

If you have completed the exercises in this chapter your communication should have improved and you may feel more confident about stating your needs, as well as asking for and giving support when it is needed. Good communication is definitely necessary to enjoy some of the content in the next chapter, which is about sexual experimentation. This contains some ideas about sexual behaviours you may be familiar with or wish to try.

Chapter Fifteen
Safe Sexual Experimentation

Being sexually adventurous may come naturally to you or be thoroughly worrying. For many of us, the idea of sexual experimentation is appealing but either seems like too much bother or we don't know where to start. There is the idea that experimentation means just finding out through play rather than planning, but it makes sense to be sure that what you're doing is as safe and healthy as possible. So this chapter has lots of ideas about sexual play and exploration. Though it does contain advice about avoiding infection and staying safe, the safety referred to in the title is really about sexual behaviour which feels comfortable and trusting, where you both feel free, unafraid, unpressured and emboldened to experiment. However, just in case you were hoping for some practical safe-sex advice, the box below contains a quick summary of some major points. There is more advice where it is relevant throughout the book.

> **SAFE SEX**
> ➤ Using a condom helps to avoid pregnancy and
>   infection. You may choose to use an additional form of
>   contraception to feel completely safe from pregnancy,
>   but never use male and female condoms together as

they tend to break each other.

➤ Use a condom and dental dams (a square of latex or silicone, see page 224) if you have, or have had, a one-night stand or an affair or are in a polyamorous relationship, as there will be an increased risk of transmitting infection even if you have no symptoms. Follow medical advice about sexual contact if an infection has actually been diagnosed.

➤ Always put on a condom before there is any contact with the penis and body, to avoid both infection and pregnancy, as sperm may be present in pre-cum.

➤ If you have herpes, avoid sex during an outbreak. Dental dams and condoms may offer protection at other times, but be aware that infected cells can be shed from the entire genital/anal area, not just the parts covered by male/female condoms.

➤ Always use a condom for anal sex. Discard the condom and, ideally, wash the penis before further vaginal or oral contact.

➤ Always use dental dams for anal-oral sex. Never reuse dental dams.

➤ Never put anything into the mouth or vagina which has been in or near the anus without very thoroughly washing the item first, and don't share anal toys. Ideally, use a condom as well.

➤ Only use a penis or sex toys for penetration of any orifice. Do not improvise with other objects, especially fruit, which can disintegrate and get stuck.

➤ Do not have intercourse with a tampon in place.

SEXUAL EXPLORATION

There may be sexual practices you are curious about or have always wanted to try, but are scared to mention to your partner. Yet the sexually naive boy or girl that you first met may now be just as ready as you are for some sexual experimentation. You may also need to appreciate that, just because you or your partner are steady and reliable in everyday life, you don't have to be that way in the bedroom too. Indeed, the predictability which might be valued in other areas of the relationship can be a distinct sexual turn-off. Why not give yourselves permission to introduce a little fun and surprise as well?

Location, location, location

For instance, sexual experiences don't always have to happen in the bedroom, or they could begin in another place. Taking a bath or shower together can be a good prelude to sex, and many couples enjoy smooching or more on a rug in front of the fire or on the sofa in front of the TV. Outdoors is exciting and different so long as you have privacy. You may find that making love in a different bedroom can also free you to behave differently too.

Some sexual experiments may have to wait until you have the house to yourselves. Like a lie-in when the children are small, there may be logistical reasons why you can't be as adventurous as you would like. Rather than blaming one another, make it part of your fantasy and something to look forward to.

Oral sex

Oral sex may be a regular part of your lovemaking, an occasional variation or something you prefer to avoid; each preference is entirely valid and normal. However, sometimes oral sex is disliked for hygiene reasons or because one of you feels self-conscious. If so, keep oral sex brief rather than making sustained efforts where you both need to concentrate. Allowing oral sex to contribute to your orgasm rather than cause it takes pressure off both of you. When there *is* pressure, managing to climax can be as much of a performance as giving oral sex and it is bound to be much less enjoyable if either of you feel stressed by the experience.

Some women who like having their genitals touched don't like having them looked at. Since oral sex brings your partner's face into contact with your vulva, you may therefore find it hard to relax. However, if your partner loves looking at your vulva, as well as kissing, sucking and nuzzling down there, the pleasure they can potentially give you is likely to please them too. Raising your bottom on a cushion or pillow and spreading your legs wide, perhaps with knees bent, will make you easier to touch, lick and kiss. Or you could lie right at the edge of the bed with your partner kneeling on the floor in front of you. Start gently and build speed and pressure gradually, whether you are making love to a man or woman.

Many men enjoy receiving teasing, licking and kissing around the head of the penis, which is its most sensitive area. Withdraw the foreskin very carefully. If you choose to put the penis in your mouth, move your mouth back and forth, focusing on the top third of the penis, using your hands to stimulate the shaft. Deeper penetration may happen in porn films but is quite difficult in real life. If you're a man enjoying oral sex, be careful about thrusting, especially if you are above your partner, as you can hurt them and make them gag.

If you are squeamish about oral sex but want to try it, do consider using a condom and/or dental dams (a square of latex or silicone) and do this anyway if there is any risk of infection. Make sure you are clean too and don't kiss your partner's mouth if your face is covered with their secretions. They *might* like it, but the chances are that they won't. Do also warn your partner before you ejaculate. They should have a choice as to whether they want to receive the ejaculate in their mouth and they should absolutely not be coerced to swallow. Some people love to swallow or to have you ejaculate over their body. But never *assume* this is okay.

Do cover your teeth with your lips. Gentle nuzzling may be fine but biting probably isn't; licking, sucking and kissing different parts of the vulva or penis are much more acceptable. Your partner should be able to guide and help you as they may like more or less pressure, gentleness or enthusiasm depending on their arousal. You may enjoy licking chocolate or cream off one another; you can buy foods especially designed for this or improvise. Beware of using foods with spices or chilli; I heard of a most unfortunate experience with guacamole!

Sex toys

If you're missing out on sex, you're probably also missing out on a whole lot of fun. When you're sexual together is probably the time that you and your partner feel able to indulge in a little relaxed silliness and there is no reason why sex toys shouldn't be a part of that. Having said this, many people see their sex toys as a vital and very serious part of their lovemaking. Either way, you can browse sex toys in shops, by mail order or online. If you haven't looked recently, you will find a vast array of goodies for singles, couples, men and women and for gay and straight sex. These include, for instance:

- Beginner's kits for anal sex (containing items such as a butt plug, lubricant and anal toys)
- Bondage gear
- Butt plugs (for additional sexual stimulation or to help prepare for anal sex)
- Condoms and dental dams
- Lingerie and dressing-up outfits
- Love balls (placed inside the vagina, they exercise the pelvic floor while stimulating the G spot)

- Male 'masturbators'
- Prostate massagers (anal vibrators which stimulate the male G spot)
- Vibrating double strap-ons for women
- Vibrators and dildos

Looking around a shop or website can be fun in itself, even when you choose not to buy anything. It may stimulate your imagination or give you confidence to try something new. It can also help to generate conversations about your sexual likes and dislikes, fantasies and desires. There is more information in the Getting Help section (see page 254).

Role play

Sex shops have always been associated with outfits for dressing up and bondage and they might provide a kick-start for role-play games. For instance, in a role play you have licence to be someone you are not. If you always wanted to be in burlesque, this is your chance. If you rather fancy yourself as a dominatrix, go for it. Naughty nurse, pilot, farmhand – you name it, there is almost certainly a costume – as long as you are a woman, that is. Sexy costumes for men are more difficult to find, though you can find outfits (fireman, doctor, soldier). However, be creative and invent some arousing scenarios and characters. It can be fun to see who turns up.

Discuss the general ground rules before you begin so that you have some idea of the 'story' or a plan for the session. Introducing the odd surprise is fine so long as it doesn't involve anything painful or distasteful to your partner. As always, they have a right to refuse. You especially need to be in full agreement if there are any bondage or domination elements to the role play. Agreeing a signal and/or word which tells the other to stop is essential, for instance.

BDSM

BDSM (which often stands for 'bondage, dominance, submission and masochism', though similar variations exist) has become much more popular among straight couples due to the recent bestselling novels involving kink and dominance. Kink in various forms was already a popular gay sexual practice, though by no means universally so. As a result of all the recent interest, there is no shortage of handcuffs, whips, chastity belts, masks and other implements to facilitate the procedure, some of which are made of rubber or leather for those with a preference or fetish.

Many of the articles are also available covered in fake fur and are clearly not intended to hurt. Because some items *could* hurt you, though, you need to be absolutely clear whether or not you want to be involved and should not allow yourself to be coerced into participating if you are at all unsure. Asking you to do something because it would prove your trust is an abuse of trust in itself. However, if you both enjoy BDSM or are curious about it, this could be a mind-blowing experiment. Do thoroughly discuss what is and is not okay and have a clear phrase or signal which tells the other to stop.

Sexual fantasy

Any of the role-play activities, whether they involve kink or not, may go better if you also learn to fantasise on your own. Though fantasy is an important part of sexual functioning, couples sometimes feel it is wrong to fantasise. For instance, you may believe that your fantasies should reflect your life with your partner. Because you may be thinking about someone else, and/or the fantasies may involve activities that you wouldn't really want to do in real life, you may feel your fantasising is a form of betrayal to your partner. Or you may think your fantasy is just wrong, especially if any form of violence is involved, such as spanking. However, the whole point of fantasy is that it is *not* real. The idea that thinking something means you want it to happen is nonsense. The mind has very cleverly given us the ability to fantasise so that we don't need to act out every single thought we have. Our most outrageous thoughts can safely remain secret.

In fantasy, not only can you have a different sexual partner but *you* can be different too. You can put yourself in situations that you would never want to experience in real life or that would be very difficult to arrange anyway. You can imagine yourself to be ultra-powerful, subjugated, more attractive, younger, older, gay, straight, a different gender, anything you like. Fantasy allows you to play with different aspects of your personality and indulge another personality altogether. If you like the idea of 17 masked blondes stimulating your nipples with a teaspoon, develop the story. Nobody ever needs to know.

There is no need to share fantasy with your partner. There may be times that you want to, especially if erotic storytelling or role play is a part of your sexual repertoire, but it is also good to keep at least some of your fantasies to yourself. Telling them can dilute them, particularly when they are very unrealistic and your partner asks questions from a position of realism.

Fantasising while making love

Just because you don't share your fantasies doesn't mean that your fantasising has to be reserved for masturbation, however. No end of people fantasise while having sex with their partner, though they may be reluctant to admit it. As was explained in the section on orgasm problems in Chapter Eleven (see page 173), fantasy can be very effectively used to help achieve a climax. Not only can the fantasy be arousing in itself, but in fantasy you can also imagine yourself to be a sexual god or goddess, with easy access to orgasms; this can sometimes help you to climax in real life. You can relive previous sexual experiences with your partner if you like, embellishing them in any way you choose. Indeed, it is a particular pleasure to be able to recall sexual encounters afterwards and allow yourself another sexual glow as you do so.

If you are one of the people who insist they are no good at fantasising, it is possible that you are not allowing yourself to let go and dream. To see whether you do have the capacity to fantasise, ask yourself the following questions.

- **Do you take pleasure in remembering generally?** If so, how hard would it be to remember a sexual encounter and add to it a little?
- **Do you ever go over events or imagine future events in your head?** This is fantasy! Unfortunately, sometimes people pay more attention to these imagined encounters than the real events – but it shows you can fantasise.
- **Have you fantasised in the past?** If you were good at making up stories or games as a child, you can still do that now.
- **Do you feel comfortable with the idea of fantasy or is it something you would deliberately avoid?** You may have been told that fantasy is wrong, but, generally, anything which helps a couple to feel closer and more bonded can only be considered useful and be encouraged.

If you have difficulty in accepting fantasy, start with one that you don't find too challenging, perhaps based on a pleasant memory of sex with your partner. You might like to begin it with a non-sexual story which establishes the setting. If you feel casual sex is wrong, you may be happier if you create a wedding-night scene or imagine lots of romance. Or you may find it easier to become aroused imagining much more dirty, raunchy sex than you normally engage in. Some people feel more comfortable if their partner stays out of the fantasies – just go with whatever feels right.

What feels right is worth thinking about. For instance, do you feel embarrassed in the fantasy? Is this part of the fun or is it inhibiting?

If you are behaving in ways that are completely different to real-life sex, does this feel liberating?

In many ways, the ability to fantasise frees you to have good sex with your partner. It is part of the process of taking responsibility for your own sexual expression and orgasm and helps to create your sexual self. If you and your partner were just the same, sex could become very dull. The more aware you are of your own sexual pleasure, and allowing yourself to express it, the more sexually interesting you are likely to become.

Fantasising does not take you away from your partner; it makes you more available to them. Even if you fantasise about someone else when you are with them, when you open your eyes you are together, sharing a magical moment, warm in each other's embrace. What could be wrong about that?

Female hot spots

Deep in the vagina, where it starts to curve upwards, is an area on the anterior (upper) wall behind the cervix which is extremely sensitive to stimulation. This is known as the A spot. Massage of this area can produce immediate copious vaginal lubrication. Continued stimulation may result in intense multiple orgasms, accompanied by powerful uterine contractions. The area probably isn't possible to stimulate with the penis, although this could be why some women particularly enjoy deep penetration. It can, however, be stimulated at the same time as the G spot. This is an area two or three inches inside the vagina on the anterior wall which becomes swollen when you are aroused. You or your partner may be able to feel a slightly spongy area, about the size of a 10-pence piece. Side to side stimulation with a couple of fingers of this or the general area can cause great pleasure in some women. It follows that a great deal of foreplay will enhance the effect of stimulating this area and it has been argued that the G spot could contribute to orgasm through intercourse.

A small area of labia on either side of the urethral opening, the U-spot, may also respond well to prolonged touch, as clitoral tissue which extends on either side of the urethra may become enlarged and responsive as arousal progresses. Indeed, it is thought that swollen clitoral tissue in all these areas is responsible for the pleasure they can produce. However, each woman's anatomy is very different. In some women, there may be less internal clitoral tissue or it may be buried more deeply and they consequently find these areas unresponsive or harder to arouse.

Some women also report finding touch in these places irritating or painful, while others claim they produce wild and different orgasmic experiences. In addition, stimulation of the U and G spots may result in female ejaculation, the production of small or large amounts of clear fluid, from a few drops to about a tablespoonful, similar in constituency to the fluid produced by the male prostate gland. Skene's glands, situated in the U-spot area of arousal are thought to produce this fluid which is sometimes distressingly confused with urine. Though it may be released via the urethra, it is definitely not urine.

Multiple orgasms

Some women can go immediately from one orgasm to the next with continued clitoral stimulation but many also need a change in pace or pressure or a short pause before being ready to begin again. Sometimes continuing clitoral touch can be uncomfortable so you need to experiment to discover what works for you. If you have had a slow build-up to your orgasm, or already had more than one, the clitoris and erogenous spots will have become swollen and extremely sensitive. Proceeding quickly to intercourse at this time may produce more orgasms through less direct clitoral stimulation and/or stimulation of the G spot. Again, you may need to experiment with the best positions to achieve this. Sometimes pelvic-floor or Kegel exercises (see pages 145 and 251) at this point, with or without a penis inside you, can also produce a series of further orgasms.

Fisting

Inserting an entire hand into the vagina or rectum is known as fisting, though the hand is not usually inserted in the shape of a fist. The fingers and hand are kept straight, with the thumb tucked in for insertion and then they are gently moved around once the hand is inside. Fingers can be used to massage the interior or the hand can be made into a fist shape and moved back and forth.

Some people very much enjoy the feeling of being filled up that this produces. It can also be used for stimulation of the prostate, A and G spots or cervix if you are very gentle. It is important to keep nails short, remove jewellery, wear latex gloves and use plenty of lube. As with all forms of penetration, it is not advisable to attempt this until arousal is well under way.

Rimming

Licking and kissing of the anal and perineal area is known as rimming. The many nerve endings around and just inside the anus can be extremely sensitive and responsive to oral touch. It can be done as a prelude to anal intercourse or alone, but may require a little planning as you will both want the area to be clean. Some people like to use an enema or mild laxative the day before to help reduce the risk of encountering faeces.

Safe sexual practice insists you use a dental dam to prevent infection. This is a square of latex or silicone used to cover the anus. Like condoms, dental dams come in a range of colours and flavours (strawberry, chocolate, mint, for instance) and can usually be bought in variety packs offering considerable choice. Alternatively, you can improvise with cling film, but this is unlikely to be as reliable. Don't turn over or reuse a dental dam and don't lick or kiss the vagina or mouth afterwards either – at least not until you have washed your face and cleaned your teeth.

Anal penetration

Many men and women, gay and straight, enjoy some form of anal penetration, whether it be with fingers, a hand, tongue, penis or sex toy. It is advisable to begin anal exploration with just a finger or tongue and avoid proceeding to anything bigger until you are used to the sensations this produces. Many people like to build up to deeper penetration over several sessions. If you are afraid or the touch hurts, the anal sphincter will clamp shut, making further exploration difficult. You may feel you want to poo at first, but this should pass as you relax and further exploration becomes possible. An internal sphincter creates a further barrier, but this will usually open with gentle massage.

Keep touch to the outside anal region rather than venturing inside if there is constipation, haemorrhoids (piles) or any cuts in the area. Even when there is no anal penetration, cuts or scratches should also be covered to prevent infection.

Don't allow/attempt penetration with sex toys or a penis until you are well aroused. Caressing the buttocks while stimulating the penis or clitoris can be very relaxing and this can continue as insertion is attempted. Penetration should be very gentle indeed, using plenty of water-based lube and, needless to say, a condom – whether you are using a penis or toy. Latex gloves and dental dams should be used as protection when touching the anal area with the fingers or mouth respectively. Penetration may be facilitated if the person being penetrated pushes slightly outwards, as though passing wind. It can also help to wear a butt plug for a few hours beforehand to relax and open the area. Resting the penis inside the rectum before thrusting begins allows the area to relax and become used to the feeling of entry.

Thrusting should be gentle, especially to begin with. Experimenting is essential to find what works for you both. A side-by-side 'spoons' position may be more comfortable than doggy-style rear entry for anal sex with a woman, as penetration is more shallow and there is access to the breasts and clitoris to facilitate stimulation. Some women like to lower themselves on to the penis facing away from the body (that is, facing the partner's feet) while many men manage face-to-face entry with the legs raised, perhaps over the penetrator's shoulders, which facilitates access to the penis.

Anal vibrators, balls, butt plugs and prostate stimulators can all be enjoyed by gay or straight men, so straight guys don't need to miss out. Indeed, there is an argument for insisting that anyone penetrating agrees to some form of anal sex beforehand so that they have an idea of what it is like.

Confidence will improve the more anal sex goes well, so do make the effort to prepare properly and agree to stop the moment either of you wants to. *Never ever* put anything that has been in or near the anus or rectum into or near a mouth or vagina. Even if you have used a condom, wash body parts and sex toys thoroughly before they are in any way used again.

Frottage

Essentially, frottage or 'dry humping' is about rubbing body parts together to produce arousal and orgasm. This can be done naked or clothed and may be arousing for both partners or only one. Clothed frottage may be something you remember from your youth, part of a dance or goodnight kiss. Purposefully indulging in clothed sex can become part of role play, be used during menstruation or when a quick encounter is required.

Frottage has a bit of a bad name, thanks to the idea that opportunistic frottage is practised in crowds by odd people. However, it can also be highly erotic and pleasurable. Genital frottage involves genitals rubbing together – penis to vagina, penis to penis, penis to anus, vagina to vagina or vagina to anus. Safe-sex precautions/ contraception may thus be required, but naked frottage can involve any part of the body. Between the thighs, armpits and between the breasts are popular variations.

Quickies

Quicky sex is a fun occasional variation which is not just for when you don't have much time. Quicky sex, naked, clothed and semi-clothed, seems to crop up a great deal in role play as it appears to be practically the only kind of sex enjoyed in Hollywood movies – frequently taking place in lifts and on kitchen tables, followed by demure reappearance in a roomful of people. Again, quicky sex may happen spontaneously, but if you hanker after quicky sex it may be helpful to let your partner know in advance. Nobody likes to feel used.

Tantra

At the other end of the speed continuum is Tantric sex. What you have probably heard or read about Tantra may have been misleading as there have been numerous modern interpretations of this ancient Indian tradition, of which Tantric sex is only a part. However it is interpreted, though, Tantric sex is basically a celebration of sexuality, using all the senses. The idea is that bodies join, harnessing and sharing energy, to raise you both into a state of spiritual awareness and profound peace. Orgasm is not the main goal and may even be seen as wasting spiritual energy. Long, languorous sex, with an emphasis on breathing, sensuality and being in the moment is very much the focus.

Many men already practise keeping themselves at a high level of arousal without climaxing, a practice known as 'edging'. The individual is aroused almost to orgasm and then stimulation is reduced or ceased and built back up again. Repeating this for many minutes or hours can induce a dreamy sense of euphoria, which has been described as spiritual.

In case you hadn't noticed, all of this is pretty much what this whole book is about. Mindfulness exercises (see pages 43 and 91) will help you to concentrate on your breathing and appreciate the here and now; sensate focus exercises (see pages 85–90) emphasise and develop sensuality and foreplay; and stop:start exercises (see pages 168–70) can keep men going without orgasm for much longer.

Of course, referring to a concept like Tantra isn't necessary to celebrate sex, as the final chapter demonstrates.

Conclusion
Celebrating Sexuality

It is terribly sad that sex and intimacy can sometimes cause so much disappointment, shame and sadness when they *could* be all about pleasure, delight, closeness and celebration. Shedding preconceptions, opening yourself up to new ideas, experiences and ways of thinking, and making an effort to communicate effectively all permit you to make the most of your relationship. To conclude the book, let's take a look at ways of honouring and celebrating your relationship and keeping the fire alive.

Ideally, physical intimacy can be a part of your everyday life, several times a day. Don't necessarily put the brakes on intimacy in front of the children. Obviously, it isn't appropriate to be sexual in front of them, but children find lots of kisses, cuddles and physical familiarity between their parents very reassuring. It is these moments which make your relationship special, so do make sure there are lots. For instance, don't be afraid to hold hands and put your arms round each other when you can, cuddle up on the sofa or enjoy a really good snog.

KISSING

Great kissing doesn't have to be a prelude to sex; if you allow it to be, kissing can even be as good for you emotionally and physically as a full-blown sexual episode. If you can relax and enjoy moments like these for themselves, they have wonderful possibilities for pleasure and intimacy. Kissing can be gentle and loving or passionate and carnal; most sexual encounters include both.

Yet kissing can provoke almost as much performance anxiety as more full-on sexual experiences. If you're going for an open kiss, do let your tongue *gently* investigate your partner's mouth. Gingerly touch tongue tips to begin with, gradually allowing the passion to develop. Don't stick a rigid tongue into your partner's mouth, however, and don't slobber.

Pay attention to the area *around* and just inside the lips, too, which is super-sensitive. Kissing the neck and throat, stroking the hair and keeping your bodies close can be comforting, intimate and arousing.

DATE NIGHTS

Many couples schedule date nights as a way of focusing on their relationship away from the pressures of work and family. Even just a quiet meal together at home once the children are in bed can be an excellent way to create couple time. Going for a night out or a weekend away is even better. *However*, date nights come with a health warning, because they have a tendency to promote unrealistic expectations and tip you right back to square one.

It is understandable that date nights are invested with a great deal of hope and expectancy, as with any celebration, so you may be hoping for sex to end the evening. However, sex may be off the menu if you don't plan your date with care. If you think back to previous date nights, you may remember feeling tense rather than excited as they approached, worrying about what could go wrong. This is often because, though they are called date nights and discussion of them suggests they should be fun, they aren't being treated like relaxing nights off. All too often, they are used as opportunities to settle scores, make plans you haven't had time for previously and to tick the sex box. However, there are ways to make the most of your evening together.

1. **Plan carefully**. Don't leave arrangements until the last minute and be clear which of you is making any bookings. Too many couples end up with nothing to do because they each assume the other is taking care of the plans or that the other ought to – but doesn't know that it's being left to them. One way of managing this is to pencil dates into the diary at the beginning of the year and take turns to be responsible for them. Make sure you know when it's your turn and book babysitters well in advance. Also make sure babysitters know how late they are expected to stay. Your evening could come to an abrupt end if your sitter calls and tells you it's time to get home. Ensure there is cash for cabs and the babysitter too, and be clear which of you is responsible for this.

2. **Leave yourselves enough time**. It isn't just hurrying home to a babysitter that can scupper the night, it's all the other commitments you have as well. For instance, you may have an early start the next day so you won't be able to go on for another drink or to a club. Do tell one another in advance what time you expect the evening to end so that neither of you ends up being disappointed.

3. **Don't use the evening to settle scores**. If you usually end up being responsible for all the arrangements, don't use your precious date night to opt out because you think it should be your partner's turn to be in charge of the plans. If they don't expect to do that, they will feel set up and humiliated and you'll have a row instead of a night out. It is far better to discuss who does what well in advance. And don't wait until you are out and then bring up all the things your partner has done wrong since the last date night. That is not what the evening is for.

4. **Stick to date conversation**. If there is anything bothering you, try to have a sit-down discussion before the evening out,

so that any problems are dealt with. This way, they won't be niggling at you and you won't be tempted to talk about them all night. An evening out to discuss problems may be a good idea, but this isn't it. This is a night for fun and enjoyment, not for making arrangements or discussing whether the bedroom needs a new carpet. Similarly, don't be tempted to talk about work, the children or pets all night. This may be what you currently enjoy most, but challenge yourselves to discuss something different. Otherwise, you may find yourselves stuck for anything to chat about when the children leave home or you retire and are facing each other alone over the dinner table.

5. **Finish the evening with a kiss**. If you *assume* the evening will end with intercourse, the chances are it will spoil the whole night if it doesn't. It is great to flirt and anticipate the way the evening *could* end. This can be a wonderful tonic to the night out. It can also spell disaster.

   If a sexual frisson lights up the evening spontaneously, and your experience of sex after nights out is generally positive, you may indeed have some sensational sex to look forward to. However, this is often what ruins a good evening. Frequently, high expectations are not rewarded as the other partner is tired or has drunk too much.

   If you agree beforehand that the evening will end with a lovely kiss and the pair of you snuggling up in bed together, you are far less likely to be disappointed. It is always possible that the kiss and cuddle will turn into something more – just don't count on it. Who knows, there may be time and opportunity for a more involved sexual encounter when you wake up in the morning. At least you won't wake with regrets and bad feeling between you.

CASE EXAMPLE: SONIA AND CRAIG

Sonia and Craig both believed that date nights were important for their relationship – but they usually ended with an argument. Craig was always worried that the evening would end badly because he would miss sexual cues, would drink too much and lose his erection or would not satisfy Sonia in some way. He was so worried about getting it wrong that he began to really dread date nights and would find himself drinking too much out of nerves.

On the other hand, Sonia always looked forward to date nights, hoping that *this* time the couple would feel some real connection and make love. However, the nights never seemed to be as romantic as she expected. She always had to make the arrangements and Craig always got drunk and either fell asleep as soon as they got home or lost his erection.

In the end, the couple agreed to avoid date nights and went for several months with no dates and no sex. Then a friend of Sonia's suggested they have activity nights instead. It was Sonia's idea to enrol in tango classes. Craig was initially reluctant to try this; even though he enjoyed dancing, he thought it would be hard work at the end of a long day. In the end, he was persuaded to give it a go. To their surprise, they both found the dancing made them feel very close and there was often an erotic charge that they had not expected – most importantly, they had fun.

Once they both realised that they were responding to one another sexually through the dancing, they noticed that other aspects of their life improved. They were less ratty with each other, talked more and felt generally better in themselves. Sometimes they made love after the tango, but they never expected to – some evenings they both just seemed to want to. Their sexual confidence increased and they found themselves initiating sex when they felt like it. They also had far more kisses and cuddles – *and* won a prize in a dance competition.

MAKING SEX SPECIAL

If your date does end with sex, or if you have planned a sex date, try to continue the sense of occasion. Don't be in too much of a hurry, otherwise it can look as if the whole evening was just a means to a sexual end rather than letting lovemaking flow from the delightful time you have had. If you can possibly remember, make sure you switch off your phone. If you need to, have a wash and clean your teeth – alcohol or coffee breath is not pleasant.

You might want to assemble contraceptives, sex toys and anything else you could need in a handy place beforehand so that you don't have to search for them at a crucial moment. However, pre-planning on the day can make it look as though sex was always your purpose, so creating a sex drawer in your bedside table now, or having a permanent known place for your bits and pieces, can avoid a sense of scheming for sex.

Keep pets out of the bedroom too and away from sex toys. A couple once brought a chewed whip to their therapy session to show what happened after their dog had decided it looked tasty. Another couple said their vibrator terrified the cat. However, it is more likely that pets will just leave you no room on the bed or whine for attention.

If you have planned the evening to coincide with a special occasion, think twice before inviting guests to stay. They are often present around birthdays and anniversaries to babysit or join your celebrations, but they may be up and waiting for you when you get home and very inhibiting when you go to bed.

Be aware that high expectations can cause performance anxiety too, so the sex may not go entirely as planned. If so, do recognise the positive intimate and sexual experiences that have gone well rather than focusing on what didn't happen.

AFTER SEX

The time immediately after sex can be as important and special as the lovemaking itself. If you can manage it, make sure you have a lovely cuddle afterwards. Less passionate kissing is also wonderful after sex. It isn't a great moment to fall straight to sleep, dash to the loo or get up to make tomorrow's lunch boxes. Even just a few minutes of cuddles and exquisite kisses is reassuring and puts a positive seal on your lovemaking. Leaving just creates insecurity and doesn't value the special time you have just had together.

Probably the most important message of this book is that most couples want an intimate relationship which includes at least some sexual expression, but not many people realistically assess how to go about it. So here are **some final tips**:

- Treat any sexual issues as a couple problem rather than the responsibility of only one of you.
- Try to be aware of your partner's sexual needs and preferences …
- … however, take responsibility for your own sexual expression.
- Don't be coerced into anything you don't want to do.
- Don't expect every cuddle to lead to intercourse.
- Enjoy cuddles and kisses for themselves rather than being disappointed when an encounter is not more sexual.

- Don't feel the number of times you have intercourse defines you sexually. Nurture your sexual image in other ways.
- Don't expect every sexual encounter to produce an orgasm.
- If things don't go as planned, work out why this happened rather than becoming anxious about it happening again.
- Don't be too serious about sex; enjoy being playful and having fun.
- Don't hanker after the early days of your relationship; your current partnership is very different.
- Appreciate what your partner does do for you, rather than focusing on what they don't do.
- Be realistic about what is possible in your circumstances and make the most of it. If this means timetabling sex, do it.
- Initiate intimate moments when the mood takes you.
- Be aware that you may need to be relaxed and free of anxiety to really make the most of an intimate sexual encounter.
- Respond to intimacy positively, but don't feel you must be sexual if you don't want to be.
- Address any problems as they occur rather than letting them build up.
- Make time for yourself *and* time for the relationship.
- Delight in your relationship, your partner, yourself.

If reading this book has helped improve your sexual expression, intimacy or relationship in any way, do congratulate yourself. Nothing can change without your willingness or without your effort. Well done!

Resources

GETTING HELP

Relate

Many people still think that Relate is an organisation for straight married people, whereas it actually helps people of all ages, from all backgrounds and all sexual orientations with their relationships. Though Relate works with individuals, children, young people and families, both in its own centres and in schools, GPs' surgeries, prisons and the community, Relate's work with couples may be of particular interest to readers of this book. Couple counselling focuses on your relationship and issues affecting it, such as improving communication, co-parenting, constant arguing, managing separation or recovery from an affair. Because of Relate's scope and because counsellors are trained to assess your needs, you may wish to use more than one service. For instance, you may initially attend for couple counselling but then choose to have some family counselling as well.

Psychosexual therapy

You can refer yourself directly for Relate psychosexual therapy or see a general couple counsellor if you aren't sure which service to book. This can sometimes happen if there are relationship problems as well or if the relationship has become more tense due to a sexual problem. All Relate's couple counsellors are trained to work with a sexual focus and are able to assess whether referral to a psychosexual therapist is appropriate. Generally, PST is more appropriate if there is a sexual dysfunction (see Chapter Eleven, pages 153–81).

Opting for psychosexual therapy from the start means you will be seen by relationship counsellors who have additional specialist training – often, a two-year masters-level diploma or four-year MSc in psychosexual therapy. The majority are trained by the Relate Institute, the professional education organisation attached to Relate. As well as Relate counsellors, students on the PST courses include health professionals from the NHS and other organisations, some coming from abroad – recently, as far afield as northern Europe, the United States and Iceland.

Arthritis
Arthritis Research UK
Has booklets and advice related to sex and arthritis
tel: 0300 790 0400
email: enquiries@arthritisresearchuk.org
www.arthritisresearchuk.org

Asperger syndrome
Different Together
Support, information and advice, including how to find a therapist, for partners of people with Asperger syndrome
www.different-together.co.uk

The National Autistic Society
Information, advice and workshops
tel: helpline – 0808 800 4104, Mon–Fri 10am–4pm
www.autism.org.uk

Bladder problems
Bladder and Bowel Foundation
Offers support and advice to people with bladder and bowel conditions
tel: helpline – 0845 345 0165; general enquiries – 01536 533 255
email: info@bladderandbowelfoundation.org
www.bladderandbowelfoundation.org

The Cystitis & Overactive Bladder Foundation
Offers advice and support
tel: advice line – 0121 702 0820
email: info@cobfoundation.org
www.cobfoundation.org

Body image
Be Real Campaign
Campaigning to change attitudes to body image and put health above appearance
www.berealcampaign.co.uk

Centre for Appearance Research
Based at the University of the West of England, the centre studies body image, shares resources and news and has research you can participate in
tel: 0117 32 82497
email: car@uwe.ac.uk
www1.uwe.ac.uk/hls/research/appearanceresearch

Cancer
Breast Cancer UK
Information and support, including several publications about sex following treatment
tel: helpline – 0808 800 6000, Mon–Fri 9am–5pm and Sat 10am–2pm
www.breastcancercare.org.uk

Jo's Cervical Cancer Trust
Information and support
tel: helpline – 0808 802 8000, check website for times the line is open
email: info@jostrust.org.uk
www.jostrust.org.uk

Macmillan Cancer Support
Information, practical and emotional help
tel: support line – 0808 808 00 00, Mon–Friday 9am–8pm
www.macmillan.org.uk
films about sex and relationships: www.youtube.com/playlist?list=
PL50568F72AE2779E4

Cardiac problems
British Heart Foundation
Information, advice and support
tel: helpline – 0300 330 3311, Mon–Fri 9am–5pm
www.bhf.org.uk/heart-health/living-with-a-heart-condition/sex-
and-heart-conditions

Chronic fatigue syndrome
ME Association
Support and information
tel: helpline – 0844 576 5326, daily 10am–12 noon, 2–4pm, 7–9pm
email: meconnect@meassociation.org.uk
www.meassociation.org.uk

Cross-dressing
Consortium
Support and advice for partners of cross-dressers
www.lgbtconsortium.org.uk/directory/transpartners

Dementia
Alzheimer's Society
Offers information and support
tel: helpline – 0300 222 11 22
www.alzheimers.org.uk

Dementia UK
Offers information and support
tel: helpline – 0845 257 9406
email: direct@dementiauk.org
www.dementiauk.org

Diabetes
Diabetes UK
Support, information and research
tel: careline – 0345 123 2399
www.diabetes.org.uk/Guide-to-diabetes/Living_with_diabetes/
Sex-and-diabetes/

Disability
Outsiders
Information and support on disability, relationships and sexuality
tel: helpline – 07074 993 527, Mon–Fri 11am–7pm
email: sexdis@outsidersorg.uk
www.outsiders.org.uk

Erectile dysfunction
Men's Health Answers
Sponsored website offering information and advice about ED
www.menshealthanswers.co.uk/erectile-dysfunction

Fertility
British Fertility Society
Practical and emotional support for infertility
tel: 01454 642 217
email: bfs@bioscientifica.com
www.britishfertilitysociety.org.uk

Infertility Network UK
Offers information and support
tel: helpline – 0800 008 7464; support line – 0121 323 5025
www.infertilitynetworkuk.com

Fibromyalgia
Fibromyalgia Association UK
Offers information and support
tel: helpline – 0844 887 2444, Mon–Fri 10am–4pm
email: charity@fmauk.org
www.fmauk.org

Herpes
Herpes Viruses Association
Information and advice
tel: 0845 123 2305
email: info@herpes.org.uk
www.herpes.org.uk

Hysterectomy
Hysterectomy Association
Information and forums
email: info@hysterectomy-association.org.uk
www.hysterectomy-association.org.uk

Irritable Bowel Syndrome
International Foundation for Functional Gastrointestinal Disorders
US-based organisation that informs, assists and supports those with IBS, including information about gynaecological aspects
www.aboutibs.org/site/signs-symptoms/gynecological-aspects

NHS Choices
Gives information on symptoms, causes, diagnosis and treatment
www.nhs.uk/conditions/irritable-bowel-syndrome/pages/introduction.
   aspx

Kegel exercises
How to feel your Kegels
film: www.youtube.com/watch?v=lwM_wwjerv8

Kegel exercises for men
www.mayoclinic.org/healthy-living/mens-health/in-depth/
   kegel-exercises-for-men/art-20045074
film: www.youtube.com/watch?v=u_zYbfdhCXg

Kegel exercises for women
www.mayoclinic.org/healthy-living/womens-health/in-depth/
   kegel-exercises/art-20045283
film: www.youtube.com/watch?v=wRKhtfbJHdo

Mindfulness
Be Mindful – Mental Health Foundation
Online mindfulness courses
bemindful.co.uk

Pelvic pain
The British Pain Society
Education, research and information
tel: 020 7269 7840
email: info@britishpainsociety.org
www.britishpainsociety.org

Endometriosis UK
Offers information and support
tel: helpline – 0808 808 2227
www.endometriosis-uk.org

Pelvic Pain Support Network
Support and information about diagnosis and treatment for those with pelvic pain, their families and carers
email: info@pelvicpain.org.uk
www.pelvicpain.org.uk

Pregnancy
NCT
Support, advice and classes. Has information on sex in pregnancy and beyond
tel: helpline – 0300 330 0700
www.nct.org.uk

Prostate
Men's Health Answers
Sponsored website offering information and advice about enlarged prostate
www.menshealthanswers.co.uk/benign-prostatic-hyperplasia

Prostate Cancer UK

Online community, information and advice about sex, relationships and prostate cancer

tel: specialist nurse helpline – 0800 074 8383

email: info@prostatecanceruk.org

prostatecanceruk.org

Psychosexual therapy

College of Sexual and Relationship Therapists

Information about psychosexual therapy and listing of therapists

tel: 020 8543 2707

email: info@cosrt.org.uk

www.cosrt.org.uk

Pink Therapy

Information and help finding therapy for lesbian, gay, bisexual and transgender individuals and others who identify with gender or sexual diversities

tel: 020 7836 6647

email: admin@pinktherapy.com

www.pinktherapy.com

Relate

Information about relationships and psychosexual therapy, plus options for counselling and local services

tel: 0300 100 1234

www.relate.org.uk/relationship-help/help-sex

Relationships Scotland

Information and local psychosexual therapy services

tel: helpline – 0845 119 2020, Mon–Fri 9am–5pm

www.relationships-scotland.org.uk

Tavistock Centre for Couple Relationships
Offers relationship and psychosexual therapy
tel: 020 7380 1960
www.tccr.org.uk

Sex toys
Ann Summers
tel: 0333 440 6969
www.annsummers.com/c/sex-toys

Lovehoney
tel: customer service – 0800 011 6899
www.lovehoney.co.uk

SexToys
tel: 08000 69 69 00
www.sextoys.co.uk

Sh!
tel: 03333 444 005
www.sh-womenstore.com

Sexual abuse
Rape Crisis
Support for women and girls who have experienced sexual violence, and access to local support agencies
tel: freephone helpline – 0808 802 9999, 12–2.30pm and 7–9.30pm
email: rcewinfo@rapecrisis.org.uk
www.rapecrisis.org.uk

The Survivors Trust
An umbrella agency, offering information on behalf of 135 specialist rape, sexual-violence and childhood sexual-abuse support organisations throughout the UK and Ireland
tel: 01788 550 554
email: info@thesurvivorstrust.org
www.thesurvivorstrust.org

Sexual compulsion
Association for the Treatment of Sexual Addiction & Compulsivity (ATSAC)
Offers information and support
tel: 07414 787 341
email: info@atsac.co.uk
www.atsac.co.uk

Relate
Offers information, advice and assessment
tel: 0300 100 1234
www.relate.org.uk/relationship-help/help-sex/sex-common-problems/
    im-worried-i-or-someone-i-know-might-be-addicted-sex

Sex Addicts Anonymous in the UK
Offers a 12-step programme for out-of-control sexual behaviours
tel: 07843 108 302
www.saa-recovery.org.uk

Sexual dysfunctions
Sexual Advice Association
Information and advice about sexual health and dysfunctions
tel: helpline: 0207 486 7262, Mon, Wed and Fri 9am–5pm
email: info@sexualadviceassociation.co.uk
www.sda.uk.net

Vulval pain

The Association for Lichen Sclerosus and Vulval Health
Offers information and advice
lichensclerosus.org

Vulval Pain Society
Information, advice and support
email: info@vulvalpainsociety.org
www.vulvalpainsociety.org

USEFUL READING

Affairs

Cole, Julia, *After the Affair: How to Build Trust and Love Again*, Vermilion (second edition, 2010)
Explores the reasons for affairs and how to repair the relationship

Asperger syndrome

Aston, Maxine, *The Other Half of Asperger Syndrome (Autism Spectrum Disorder): A Guide to Living in an Intimate Relationship with a Partner who is on the Autism Spectrum*, Jessica Kingsley Publishers (paperback, second revised edition, 2014)
Information and advice for couples

Body image

Hutchinson, Marcia Germaine, *Transforming Body Image: Learning to Love the Body You Have*, Crossing Press (2001)
Exercises and information to change your self-image

Orbach, Susie, *Bodies*, Profile Books (2010)
An exploration of how our view of our bodies affects our self-image

Fantasy

Friday, Nancy, *My Secret Garden*, Quartet (2001)
 The first major collection of women's sexual fantasies

Men and sex

Zilbergeld, Bernie, *The New Male Sexuality*, Bantam Books (revised edition, 1999)
 Author's findings from 20 years as a psychologist specialising in human sexuality, as well as those from other experts in the field

Menopause

Brayne, Sue, *Sex, Meaning and the Menopause*, Continuum (2011)
 An in-depth look at the effects of menopause and ageing and how they can be managed

Mindfulness

Alidina, Shamash, *Mindfulness for Dummies*, John Wiley & Sons (second edition, book and CD, 2014)
 A practical guide, including techniques, meditations and exercises

Sexual compulsion

Carnes, Patrick, Delmonico, David and Griffin, Elizabeth, *In the Shadows of the Net: Breaking Free from Compulsive Online Sexual Behavior*, Hazelden Information and Educational Services (second revised edition, 2007)
 Information and strategies for managing internet addiction
Hall, Paula, *Understanding and Treating Sex Addiction*, Routledge (2013)
 Explains why and how sexual addiction develops, its effect on relationships and how it can be treated
Weiss, Robert, *Cruise Control: Understanding Sex Addiction in Gay Men*, Alyson Books (second edition, 2005)

Recognising, treating and recovering from sexual addiction, as well as recovery in the primary relationship for gay men

Thinking

Greenberger, Dennis and Padesky, Christine A. *Mind Over Mood: Change How You Feel By Changing the Way You Think*, Guilford Press (1995); www.mindovermood.com

A workbook designed to be used alone or in conjunction with professional treatment

Index